Asia

lonely planet

phrasebooks

Central Asia phrasebook
2nd edition – July 2008

Published by
Lonely Planet Publications Pty Ltd ABN 36 005 607 983
90 Maribyrnong St, Footscray, Victoria 3011, Australia

Lonely Planet Offices
Australia Locked Bag 1, Footscray, Victoria 3011
USA 150 Linden St, Oakland CA 94607
UK 2nd floor, 186 City Rd, London, EC1V 2NT

Cover illustration
Every Little Thing She Does is Tajik by Brendan Dempsey

ISBN 978 1 74059 114 0

text © Lonely Planet Publications Pty Ltd 2008
cover illustration © Lonely Planet Publications Pty Ltd 2008

10 9 8 7 6 5 4 3 2

Printed through The Bookmaker International Ltd.
Printed in China

acknowledgments

about the author

Justin Jon Rudelson grew up in Beverly Hills, California. In his teens he set out to become a Confucian Jew, a journey that led him to study Mandarin and eventually twenty other languages including Uyghur, Uzbek, Russian, Japanese and Hebrew.

In his Asian Studies work at Dartmouth College and while earning a doctorate in Social Anthropology at Harvard University, he studied over four years in China and Central Asia, the majority in Xinjiang, China. His book on the Uyghurs is entitled *Oasis Identities: Uyghur Nationalism along China's Silk Road* (Columbia University Press, 1997).

He also interpreted for the Chinese and Taiwan track and field teams at the Olympics in 1984 and 1996, worked as a photographer and journalist on assignments on Central Asia for *National Geographic*, and helped introduce drip irrigation technologies from Israel into China's deserts.

dedication

This book is dedicated to Auden and Trillin, my sons.

from the author

I thank Sally Steward for her friendship, patience, enthusiasm and vision. She brought a wild dream to reality, made me feel part of the LP team by bringing the USA's down under (Louisiana) closer to the universe's down under (Australia) through upbeat email, and even music from her native New Zealand to inspire me. My great appreciation also goes to phrasebook editor Peter D'Onghia, who did the mind-bending, nitty gritty work of filling holes in phrases, overseeing language map production, and shepherding this book through completion. A special debt of gratitude is extended to Zita Felfoldi, who was responsible for the tedious task of transcribing the handwritten entries with painstaking accuracy as they came in from all over the world.

Linguist Ablät Sämät was most instrumental in writing the Kyrgyz section, correcting my insufficient Uyghur, and locating Märpugha Neghemet to write the Kazakh section and Ghalip Zulal to write the Tashkorghàni section. The Pashto section was written by Pakistani scholar Obaidullah Asad, who was located in Beijing while doing a stint as the Pashto language news broadcaster for Radio China.

Dinara Amanbekova, a Kyrgyzstani psychologist, enthusiastically volunteered to transform Chinese Kyrgyz to that spoken in Kyrgyzstan. For Kazakh, anthropologist Cynthia Werner, who spent over two years in a rural town in Kazakhstan, shifted the East Turkestani dialect to that of Kazakhstan.

A Tulane University colleague, Anne McCall, found Ogulsona Ishankuliyeva to write the Turkmen section. Her work was supplemented by David Tyson, a scholar of the Turkmen language. Finally, Noor Umarov wrote the Tajik section while finishing his finals in California, and Jahangir Kakharov also balanced phrases with exams. To all of these authors, may your labours bring glory to the lands and peoples that you hold so dear.

from the publisher

This book was edited by Peter D'Onghia, with editorial assistance from Branislava Vladisavljevic and Laura Crawford. Sally Steward oversaw production and made many valuable editorial suggestions. Penelope Richardson designed and, along with Katherine Marsh, laid-out the book. Han Than Tun did the illustrations and Brendan Dempsey created the cover. Jacqui Saunders, Paul Clifton and Wayne Murphy supplied the maps. Ben Handicott, Karin Vidstrup Monk, Rachel Williams, Yukiyoshi Kamimura, and Annelies Mertens also contributed in various ways.

John King compiled the Burushashki, Kohistani, Mandarin, Shina, Kohistani, Wakhi sections and with Bradley Mayhew, the Khowar. The Mongolian and Russian were compiled at Lonely Planet.

CONTENTS

Introduction

INTRODUCTION

One of the most fascinating aspects of Central Asia is its languages. The Central Asian languages are principally divided between those classified as Turkic (such as Kazakh, Kyrgyz, Turkmen, Uyghur and Uzbek) and those related to Persian (like Tajik and Pashto), thus included in the huge Indo-European family of languages which includes English.

A distinction should be made between Turkic and Turkish. While Turkish is one language, Turkic is a language family that includes Turkish as well as those mentioned above.

Many Central Asians, especially those in Uzbekistan and Tajikistan, speak both Turkic and Persian languages. Persian grammar is similar to the major Indo-European languages so it is relatively easy to learn. Knowledge of Latin grammar will help to some degree, since, like Latin, Turkic verbs also are placed at the end of the sentence. Learning Turkic dialects is enjoyable because they are highly expressive, a feature greatly magnified by most Central Asians who whine when they speak. Yes, whining is sometimes a must.

As one travels throughout the Turkic heart and periphery of Central Asia it becomes abundantly clear that the Turkic languages are really dialects of one another and not distinct languages at all. This means that in learning one, all the rest are understandable to a large degree. Herein lies the fun and the challenge.

Speaking the native languages of Central Asia to any degree will be tremendously appreciated by the local people. It will also increase your mobility and access to the various Central Asian cultures. Very few of the inhabitants of even the major Central Asian cities speak western languages, though many do know Russian or Mandarin depending on their colonial legacy. Attempting to speak any local words is greeted with an outpouring of warmth. Central Asians are incredibly hospitable so be prepared upon uttering a simple yakhshimu siz? 'How are you?' to be invited into a family home and be served tea, sweets and cakes.

HISTORICAL ORIGINS

It's a common misunderstanding that the Turkic languages emanated from present day Turkey. In fact, the Turkic languages developed with the Turkic Empire in the 6th century. The Turkic people, who were centered in Mongolia, spread their influence east and west. The Uyghur Empire (745 to 840 AD) developed in Mongolia and was the first nomadic empire to have its own writing system. Uyghur scribes and scholars would later become the major advisors to Jenghiz (Genghis) Khan and the Mongol Empire. The Turks spread their influence to the west and into Iran.

Prior to the year 1000 AD, the lingua franca of Central Asia was Persian. Turkic dialects, though spoken in the Central Asian oases and villages, had not yet been accepted by elite society. But by 1000 AD, this began to change and within two hundred years, Central Asia was principally using Turkic for communication to the detriment of the Persian language. How this happened is still not completely known. It was as late as the 11th century that Turkic tribes moved into the Anatolian peninsula, today's Turkey. Thus, Turkey was one of the last stops of Turkic civilization, not its origin.

The over 70 existing Turkic languages were delineated during the tsarist Russian conquest of Central Asia beginning in the 1860's. The tsars, and later the Soviets, magnified the minor linguistic differences between the Central Asians, who did not see themselves as separate people, to differentiate the Central Asians into numerous ethnic people speaking different languages. This is not to say that there were no distinctions. Turkic is divided into four main dialects:

1. eastern dialects of the Altay region near the Chinese border with former Soviet Central Asia
2. western dialects of the Kyrgyz and Tatar
3. dialects of Western Turkestan
4. southern dialects of the Turkmen, the Azeris, and the Anatolians

INTRODUCTION

In late tsarist and early Soviet Russia, distinct republics were created from linguistic lines that were faint and faded at best. In the early years of the Soviet empire during Lenin's leadership, a young Josef Stalin led the ethnic definition project in 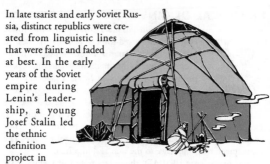 Central Asia that drew the borders. The legacy of divide and rule is still exerting its influence especially since the independent Central Asian nations inherited their Soviet-drawn borders. In your travels through Central Asia and in using a few of the various dialects you'll discover how faint the differences truly are between the Turkic people.

VARIETIES OF CENTRAL ASIAN LANGUAGES

The Persian and Turkic languages which form the core of Central Asian languages are spoken by more than 250 million people. The Turkic languages are spoken from Macedonia to Siberia and China. The Persian languages are spoken in Iran, Afghanistan, Central Asia and into China. The major languages covered in this book are spoken in Afghanistan, Kazakhstan, Kyrgyzstan, Pakistan, Tajikistan, Turkmenistan, Uzbekistan and Xinjiang Province, China. At the end of this book we have included 10 other languages that will come in handy in your travels.

Rather than employing the various scripts used for the languages in their home countries, we've attempted to use a unified script employing the Roman alphabet and based on a modified transliteration system commonly used for Turkic and Persian languages.

The Turkic languages are based on the ideal of vowel harmony, in that a word should contain either the vowels formed in the front of the mouth (ä, ö, ü) or the vowels formed in the back of the mouth (a, e, i, o, u), but not both types. The Turkic dialects have a melodious quality due to the use of front vowels, as is clear in the words tünügün (Uyghur for 'yesterday') and körüdösüngör (Kyrgyz for 'you (pl) are seeing').

Although both Pashto and Tajik belong to the Persian (Iranian) family of languages, Pashto is an eastern Persian language while Tajik is a south-west Persian language. They, subsequently, have a few differences.

While they are both SOV languages, Unlike Tajik, Pashto has grammatical gender, and number in nouns. Adjectives, in Pashto, normally come before the noun and agree in number and gender with the noun they describe.

LANGUAGE ESSENTIALS

There are always essential words you need to know in a language. In Turkic there are the all-purpose greetings:

yakhshimu siz?	How are you?
qandaq/qanday?	What's happening?

When you say yakhshimu siz? and shake hands at the same time, the unique Central Asian handshake should be used. Your hands are held out close together and your right hand slides between the other's hands while your left hand rests on top of the other's right hand. It forms a hand sandwich or a four-hand layer cake with alternating layers. The slide in is performed very gently and hands only lightly touch. There is no firmness in the hands and no grabbing. After the hands slide in, pull back your hands open palmed and draw them towards your eyes and nose, and then pull them downward as if stroking a beard, imagined or real. This same beard-stroking gesture is made when completing a meal or finishing study of the Koran. It is without a doubt one of the most beautiful gestures you will experience in your lifetime.

INTRODUCTION

'Yes' is **hä'ä**, and 'no' is **yaq**. When you say **yaq** you can whine and grimace a little for a good effect, especially if it is about something particularly disgusting. 'Thank you' is **rakhmät** and to express heartfelt thanks hold your right hand over your heart and give a modest bow. 'Goodbye' is **hosh**, which literally means 'happiness' and is said with the same heart holding and bowing. This gesture's beauty comes close to the handshake but beware for it is highly addictive and you may find yourself continuing to do it even after you have returned to your native country.

ABBREVIATIONS USED IN THIS BOOK

coll	colloquial	pl	plural
f	feminine	pol	polite
inf	informal	lit	literally
m	masculine	sg	singular

Uyghur

UYGHUR

INTRODUCTION

The Uyghur language is spoken by over eight million people, the majority of whom, nearly 7.5 million, are the Uyghurs living in Xinjiang Province, China, also known as East Turkestan or Uyghuristan. Like the Uzbeks, the Uyghurs are sedentary oasis dwellers who live along the southern and northern routes of the Silk Road, along which they acted as the go-betweens of cultural exchange between the civilisations of China, India, Central Asia, Europe, and the Middle East.

As Sino-Soviet relations fell apart in 1962, the Uyghur inhabitants of north-west Xinjiang fled to Kazakhstan (over 200,000), Kyrgyzstan (around 40,000) and Uzbekistan (around 40,000). There's also a small community of Uyghurs living in Taiwan, who left Xinjiang in 1949 with Chiang Kaishek's Nationalist forces. Small groups of Uyghurs live in the USA, Germany and Turkey.

The Uyghur language is written in a modified Persian-Arabic script with distinct vowel letters in China and a Cyrillic script in Kazakhstan and Kyrgyzstan. Prior to 1978, the Chinese government imposed changes to a Cyrillic script and later to a Roman script based on their pinyin writing system. The transliteration system used in this phrasebook for all languages is a modified form of the Roman pinyin system.

PRONUNCIATION

Most Uyghur sounds are also found in the English language while a few additional ones must be learned. Intonation is important and this can be learned by listening to Uyghurs speak. You will learn quickly that it's imperative to whine while speaking Uyghur.

Vowels

There are eight vowels in the Uyghur language and almost all correspond to English sounds, except the sounds ö and ü, which are produced with rounded lips.

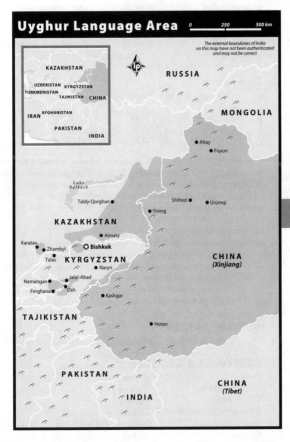

Uyghur Language Area

0 250 500 km

The external boundaries of India on this map have not been authenticated and may be correct

UYGHUR

a	as in 'father'
ä	as in 'hat'
e	as in 'bet'
i	as in 'bill'
o	as in 'go'

ö	as the 'e' in 'her', said with well rounded lips
u	as in 'put'
ü	as the 'i' in 'bit', said with rounded and pushed forward lips

Consonants

h	with aspiration as in 'haste'
j	as in 'jar'
p	slightly muffled as in 'push'
q	a hard 'k' as in the Arab country 'Qatar'
r	slightly trilled, soft, and close to an 'l' sound

The consonants written with two letters (cluster) are fairly easy to learn. The ch and sh are found in English. The four other clusters will take practice but if they are too difficult in the beginning you can pronounce the gh as an 'r', the kh as an 'h', and zh like a 'j' and you'll eventually be understood.

ch	as in 'cheek'
gh	similar to the French 'r' – produced by moving the bulk of the tongue backwards to constrict the air flow in the pharynx, while the tip of the tongue rests behind the lower front teeth. It's similar to the noise made by some people before spitting, but with less friction.
kh	a slightly guttural sound like in the Scottish 'loch'
ng	as the 'ng' in 'sing'
sh	as the 'sh' in 'sheep'
zh	as the 's' in 'vision' and 'treasure'

GREETINGS & CIVILITIES

Please.	märhämät
Please sit down.	olturung
Thank you.	rähmät sizgä
Excuse me/Pardon me.	kächürüng
Never mind.	keräk yoq (hichqisi yoq)
Correct.	toghra

Good.	yakhshi
OK.	maqul
That will do.	bolidu
Do you understand?	chüshändingizmu?
No.	yaq
Yes.	hä'ä/shundaq
I understand.	chüshandim
I don't understand.	chüshänmaymän/chüshänmidim
Sorry.	kächürüng
No problem.	chataq yoq
Please wait awhile.	biraz saqlap turung
Where's the toilet?	hajätkhana qäyärdä?

UYGHUR

The Uyghurs have different forms of greetings for men and women. The polite form of greeting for men is to place your right hand on your heart and bow slightly. Men who are more acquainted shake hands by gently placing their hands, thumbs up, in between each other's with the right hand of one touching the outside of the other's left and each's left hand sandwiched between the other's hands. After the hands touch slightly, one brings one's hands in an outward circular motion towards the mouth and then brings the hands downward. This same motion is used when saying prayers over food.

Women bow slightly toward men and toward each other but they don't make contact through handshakes or cheek kissing.

Greetings & Goodbyes

Good morning/day/evening.	ässalamu äläykum
	(lit: peace be upon you)
And upon you be peace.	wä'äläykum ässalam
Good night.	yakhshi chüsh körüng
How are you?	qandaq ahwalingiz?
How is your health?	salamätligingiz qandaq?
Fine (and you?)	yakhshi (siz chu?)
Not bad.	yaman emes

UYGHUR

Have you eaten?	tamaq yidingizmu?
Where are you going?	nägä barisiz?
What are you doing?	nimä kiliwatisiz?
Goodbye.	her khosh/khosh
See you tomorrow.	ätä körüshäyli
I wish you a good trip.	sizgä aq yol tiläymän
See you again later.	yänä körüshämiz
You've been a great help.	siz nahayiti zor yardäm qildingiz

- Uyghurs use several sounds to indicate intention and meaning. When indicating distance they raise the pitch of their voices. For example, to say that Japan is over in that direction and is very far, one would do so by elongating the word uyerde ('over there') and speak as if squealing at a high pitch.
- The frequently heard sound whey or whoa is the sound used to attract attention or annoyance with one's action. When Uyghurs try to clear a path in a crowd they shout posh, posh.
- Disgust is indicated by making a clicking sound before the word 'no', yaq, or by the sound wää. A clicking sound accompanied by a head shake signifies disapproval or pity. Clicking may also express surprise, wonder, or bitterness.
- The greeting yakhshimusiz and the reply yakhshi as well as the greeting ässalamu äläykum and the reply wä'äläykum ässalam can be used for all occasions. The phrases khosh and her khosh are appropriate conversation endings.
- Uyghur men beckon people with the ubiquitous whoa sound. Sometimes it's accompanied by an elaborate arm motion that resembles swatting a bee. A higher pitch whey sound indicates happiness.

LANGUAGE DIFFICULTIES

Do you speak English?	siz englizchi sözliyalaysiz?/
	siz englizchä sözliyälämsiz?
What languages do you speak?	siz nimätil sözläysiz?/
	siz qaysi tildä?

I speak (English) and (German).	män (englizchi) bilan (germaniyächi) sözläymän
I don't speak English.	män englizchä sözliyalmäymän
I don't speak Uyghur.	män uyghurchä sözliyalmäymän
I don't speak Chinese.	män khänzuchä sözliyalmäymän
Do you have an interpreter?	siz terjiman barmu?
How do you say that in Uyghur?	buni uyghurchidä nimä däp ataysiz?
Can you repeat that please?	yänä bir ketim däng?
Could you speak louder/ slower please?	(yukururak awazi bilän)/ (astarak) sözlung, bolamdu?
Please point to the phrase in the book.	mawu kitap ichidin bu sözni körsütüp
Just a minute.	bir däm turung
What does it mean?	uning mänisi nimä?

SMALL TALK
Meeting People

People nod to one another when a friend or relative is approaching from a distance away, or if they are passing each other in a hurry and aren't able to stop to say hello. It's polite and normal to ask about the health of someone else's parents and family and about the other person's health. Often people ask tenchlikmu? ('Are you at peace?').

People attract a stranger's attention by yelling out wey yoldash ('hey comrade'). For someone they know they call out wey and the person's name or, depending on the relative ages of both parties, one might yell out aka ('brother'), acha ('sister') or other familiar terms.

What's your name?	ismingiz/etingiz nimä?
What's your father's name?	atanizning eti nimä?
Who are you?	siz kim bolisiz?
I'm pleased to meet you.	siz bilän körüshim üchün nahayiti khushalmän

So am I.	män mu khushal
What time is it?	sa'ät qanchä boldi?
What's this?	bu nimä?
Are your parents alive?	ata aningiz bar mu?
My (mother) is alive but my (father) is not.	(apam) bar, lekin (atam) yoq

Nationalities

The first questions Uyghurs ask foreign travellers are the country dölät where they are from, their nationality or ethnic group millät , their religion din , their name and their occupation.

What country do you come from?	siz qäysi dölätdin keldingiz?
What ethnic group do you come from?	siz qäysi millät?
I'm (American).	män (amerikalik)

Age

Uyghur men in particular often look older than they are because of the dry harsh climate of Xinjiang. Foreign men with beards are often thought to be very old because Uyghur, Hui and Han men alike don't grow beards until their 30s and 40s.

How old are you?	siz qanchä yäshqa kirdingiz?
How old do you think I am?	mini qanchä yäshqa kirdi däp?
I think you are (35) years old.	(ottuz bäsh) yäshqa kirdi däp oylayman

Religion

Uyghurs are very curious about the religion of foreign travellers. You might be asked point blank what religion you believe in and which prophet, payghamber , you follow. According to Islam, Moses (musa) is the prophet of Judaism, Jesus (esa) the prophet of Christianity, and Muhammad the prophet of Islam.

I am (a) ...	man ...
Buddhist	budda'i
Catholic	katolik
Christian	kristiyan

Confucian	kongzi sishiangjia
Hindu	hindu
Jewish	yehudi
Muslim	musulman

I'm not religious (at all).	män (hichbir) dingha ishenmäymän
Do you attend Mosque?	siz mechitkä baramsiz?
I attend Mosque every Friday.	män her juma kuni mechitkä bariman

UYGHUR

Family

This is my ...	bu mining ...
father/mother	atam/apam
husband/wife	irim/ayalim
girlfriend/boyfriend	muhabbätim
son/daughter	oghulim/qizim (hammam)
younger brother/sister	inim/singlim (yängäm)
older brother/sister	akam/acham (hädäm)

Are you married?	siz toy qildignizmu?
I'm married.	män toy qildim
How many children do you have?	nächä baligniz bar?
I don't have any children.	män däbala yoq
How many brothers/sisters do you have?	siz nächä aka-uka/acha-singlingiz bar?
I don't have any brothers/sisters.	män akam/acha-singil yoq

GETTING AROUND

I'd like to go to ...	män ... barmaqchimän
How can I get to ...?	män ... gha qandaq baralimän?
Which (bus) do I take to get to ...?	män qäysi (aptobus) bilan ... gha baraliman?
Is there another way to get there?	bashqa amal barmu?

What time does the next ... leave/arrive?	kilär qetim qisi ... qachan mangidu/yitip baridu?
bus	aptobus
train	poyiz
plane	ayrupilan

Where is the ...?	... qäyärdä?
airport	ayrudurum
bus stop	aptobus bikiti
(long distance) bus terminal	(uzunyolluq) aptobus bikiti
train station	poyiz istanzisi
ticket office	belät satidighan jay (belät setish orni)

Is it far?	yiraqmu?
Yes, it's far.	hä'ä, yiraq
It's quite close.	u nahayiti yeqin
Can I walk there?	mushu yerdin awu yargichä mangishga bolamdu?

How much time will it take to walk there?	piyadä yürse, qanchilik wakit kitidu?
What's the address?	uning adresi qandaq?
Please write down the address for me.	manga uning adresini yezip bering
Could you tell the taxi driver the address please?	kira mashinisi (taksi) hopurigha bu adresini ay tip bärsingiz?
Please draw a map for me.	manga khäritisim sizip biring

UYGHUR

Directions

Uyghurs are reliable when it comes to giving directions to tourists but it's always best to reconfirm directions by asking someone else along the way. If they don't know, they'll usually tell you, and in the east and Urümqi the Han word 'tang' is sometimes used to mean 'I don't know.'

Which direction?	qaysi yünülüshtä?
that direction/this direction	u/bu täräp
Go straight ahead.	aldigha udul mangmaq
Turn right/left.	onggha/solgha burulush

east/west	shärq/ghärp
north/south	shimal/jänup
southeast/northwest	(shärqi janup)/(ghärbi shimal)
uphill/downhill	tagh üsti/baghri
left/right	sol/ong
up/down	üsti/töwän (töwänki qisim)
upstairs/downstairs	(üstinki qäwät)/(astinqi qäwät)
at the corner	burulush
far away	yiraq (yiraqta)
inside/outside	ichidä(ichkirisidä)/sirtida
middle	ottur (otturisi)
near/near to ...	yeqin/yeqinda ...

Buying Tickets

Where's the ticket office?	belät satidighan jay qäyärdä?
I'd like a (1st class) ticket to (Korla).	mänga (korla)gha baridighan (birinchi qetimliq) ning biliti lazim
How much is the train to (Ili)?	(ili)-gäbaridighan poyizning belät bahasi qanchä?
Is there a ticket for the bus to (Kashgar) today?	bügün (qäshqärgä) baridighan aptobusning belät bar mu?
What's the cheapest fare to (Ili)?	(iligä) ang arzan belät qäysi?
There are no tickets.	belät yoq

berth number	orun numuri
cancelled	bikar qilish
confirm	muäyyänlüshtürmäk (okäy oyildurmug)
dormitory bunk	yataq karwiti

UYGHUR

economy class	iqtisadiy bölüm
1st class	birinchi därijilik bölüm
2nd class	ikkinchi därijilik
one-way ticket	täq yolluq bilät
return tickets	berip kilish biliti
refund	pul tölimük
seat	orun
student ticket	oqoghuchi biliti
ticket office	belät satidighan jay
timetable	waqit jädwili

Air

There are flights to many of the oases from Urümqi. Recently the Xinjiang airline has been renting planes from Aeroflot and so you shouldn't be surprised if the pilot is a blonde-haired Russian. Airports in Xinjiang are fairly good and able to accommodate large jets. Kashgar is serviced by planes that carry more than 150 passengers.

| I want to confirm my flight. | bilitimni okäy qildurimän |
| This price is higher than normal. | bu bahu adüttikidin üstün |

aeroplane	ayrupilan
airline ticket	ayrupilan biliti
customs' (declaration)	haigüän (mälumuti)
departure	ayrilish
estimated time of arrival/	(yetip birishi)/(yolgha chiqishi)
departure	üchün mölgärlangän waqti
gate number	eghiz/ishik numuri
no smoking	tamaka chikishkä bolmaydu
passport	passport

Bus

Buses in Urümqi are very crowded, as in most of China. In winter, since no salt or dirt is used to melt ice, buses crawl at 15 km per hour.

Long-distance bus travel is the cheapest but also the most gruelling. *Remember:* sit up the front unless you want to sit in the back and be bounced up so high your head hits the ceiling. The seats are not padded well enough for re-entry. The bus will stop if a traveller has to go to the bathroom. Here the desert is your WC. When getting off

for group pit stops, men will go to one side and women another.
Everyone squats to inhibit being seen by those of the other sex.

Is this going to the (bazaar)?	bu (bazaar)gha barmamdu?
I want to get off at ...	man ...dä chüshimän
Please tell me when we've reached that stop.	u bikätkä qächan yitip baridighanlighini manga eytip bärsingiz

bus (terminal)	aptobus(ning akhirqi bikiti)
long-distance bus station	uzun yolluq aptobus bikiti

Train

For trains leaving Xinjiang to China proper, the roughest ride is the
hard bench. Here you'll be pressed against the masses but will make
a lot of new friends. Soft seats and hard sleepers are the next best
ride and have fewer people crowding around. Soft sleepers put you in
cabins of four people. Beware of ceiling fans on the upper bunks that
tend not to protect against digits and limbs hitting the blades.

Can you help me find my seat/berth please?	ornimni tepiwelishim üchün yardäm berälämsiz?
Excuse me, this is my seat.	kächürüng, bu mining ornum
Where is the dining car?	tamaqhana wagoni qayärdä?

dining car	poyiz tamaqhanisi
(express) fast train	(alahide) tiz poyiz
hard seat/sleeper (2nd class)	qattiq uruunduq/karwat
soft-seat (1st class)	yumshaq karwat
train	poyiz

Taxi

Taxis are relatively easy to find in Urümqi, and very easy to get at
hotels. All taxis have meters in Urümqi. In the oases, taxis are found
closer to hotels and prices need to be negotiated.

I'd like to go to ...	män ...-gä barmaqchimän
How long does it take to go to ...?	... ke berishqa qanchilik waqit kitidu?

Are any English-speaking drivers available?	englishchä sözliyäläydighan shopur barmu?
How much?	qanchä pul?
Please stop here.	bu yärdä tokhtang
Stop at the next corner.	yänä bir dokhmushta tokhtang
Please hurry.	tizräk bolung
Please slow down.	sür'ätni astiliting
Please wait here.	bu yärdä saqlang
I'll get off here.	män mushu yärdä chushimän
Where can I hire a taxi?	qayärdin täksi ijarigä alalaymän?
How much is it for one/three day(s)?	bir/üch künlügi qanchä pul?

Useful Words

accident	hadis
air-conditioning	hawa tängshighüch
battery	batariyä
bicycle	wälsipit
brake	tormuz
car	mashina/pik up
insurance	istira khuaniya
(international) driving licence	(khälqära) shopurluq kinishkisi
engine oil	aptol
fill up	toldurush jalash
flat tyre	rezinkä chaq
headlight	aldi chiraq
highway	yoquri sürätlik tash yol
map	khärite
motorbike	motosikilit
parking	tokhtutush
petrol	binzin (yeqilghu meyi)
radiator	radiator
taxi stand	täksi bikiti
service station	mulazimät orni
towing a car	mashinini söräsh
tyre	chaq

UYGHUR

ACCOMMODATION

hotel/inn	mihmanhana
apartment	bina
dormitory	yataq
guesthouse	saray mihmanhana öyi
youth hostel	yashlar mihmanhanisi

It's rare to find accommodation with a Uyghur family as it's a political risk for a Uyghur to put up a foreign guest. Hotels and guesthouses come in a variety of qualities. Prices for a long-term stay can be negotiated especially if you're willing to start language courses for the staff.

Where's a guesthouse?	mihmanhana qayärdä?
I'd like to book a room.	män bir öy keräk
I'm looking for a ... hotel.	män ... mihmanhana izlewatimän
cheap	ärzan
clean	pakiz
good	yakhshi
near-the-city	shäharning yenida
near-the-airport	ayrudurmning yenida
nearby	yeqin yiridä

Booking a Room

Do you have any rooms available?	bikar öyünglar barmu?
Do you have any beds available?	bikar karwitinglar barmu?
I'd like a ...	manga bir yalghuz kishilik ... keräk
single/twin room	bir/ikki kishilik öy
quiet room	tinch öy
big room	chong öy
(double) bed	(ikki kishilik) karwat

At the Hotel

How much is it per night/person?	bir kichiligi/kishilik qanchä pul?
Is there a discount for students/children?	oqughuchi/balilargha bahada itiwar?

UYGHUR

Can I get a discount if I stay longer?	uzaqraq tursam bahada itiwar büräm siz?
Are there any cheaper ones?	ärzanraqidin birärsi barmu?
Can I see the room first?	däsläp öyni körsäm bulamdu?
Are there any others?	bashqisi barmu?
I like this/that room.	män bu/shu öyni amraq
It's fine, I'll take this room.	bu bulidikän, män mushu öyni alay

I'm going to stay for ...	män ... turmaqchi
one/two night(s)	bir/ikki kichä
a few days	bir nächä kün
a week	bir häptä

Can I have the key please?	achquchni manga birämsiz?
Is hot water available all day?	issiq su dawamliq barmu?
Could I have a different room?	bashqä öy alsam bolamdu?
Any messages/faxes for me?	manga khäwiri/faks barmu?
Please do not disturb.	däkhli qilmang

Requests & Complaints

It's too ...	bu bakhmu ... qaptu
big/small	chong/kichik
cold/hot	soghoq/qizziq (issiq)
dark/dirty	qarangghu/mäynät
noisy	warang-churung

It smells.	bu purap qaptu
The toilet/sink is blocked.	oburni/yundäeriqi itilip qaptu
The door is locked.	ishik taqilip (itilip) qaptu
My room number is (123).	öy numurum (bir yüz yigirmä üch)
Please fix it as soon as possible.	buni tizräk ornitip barsingiz

Checking Out

I'd like to check out now/ tomorrow	män hisawat qilimagchimän hazir/ätä
I'd like to pay the bill.	män talungha pultölimakchiman

Can I leave my bags here for a few days? — män somkalarni bu yärdä bir nächä kün qoyup tursam bolumdu?

Thank you for your hospitality. — mihmandostlighingiz üchün rähmät

I'm returning ... — män ... qaytiman
tomorrow — ätä
in 2-3 days — ikki-üch kündä
next week — kilär häptä

Useful Words

address	address	hot water	issiq su
bag	somka	key	achquch
basin	das	laundry	kirhana
bathroom	muncha hana	lift/elevator	lift
bed	karwat	light bulb	lampuchka
bill	talun	lobby	karidor
blanket	adiyal	lock	qulup
bucket	chiläk	luggage	yük -taqa
door	ishik	room	öy
electricity	tok	shower	dush
fan	yälpügüch	toilet	oburni (hali jay)
heating	kizitish		

UYGHUR

AROUND TOWN

Urümqi, the capital of Xinjiang, is a modern city of a million and a half residents, only 20% of whom are Uyghurs. The city is typical of those in China proper and doesn't have a Central Asian feel. The outlying oases of Xinjiang are another matter. Dotting the outskirts of the Täklimakan Desert, the second largest desert in the world, the colours of the oases, the reddish mud homes, green foliage and dusty tree-lined streets are welcoming variations to the monotonous desert landscape. Central bazaars explode with colour and activity. Uyghur women stroll the streets in multicoloured silk skirts and nylon stockings, their gold earrings dangling, and call out to one another in high-pitched tones. Uyghur men, in square brimless skull-caps, shout at friends with a whining whoa sound. Some prepare shish kebabs, adding to the heavy smell of spices and smoke in the marketplace.

Old bearded Uyghur men, in turbans and knee-high black leather boots, answer the call to prayer, donkey carts bounce through dust-filled lanes, their drivers cracking whips, yelling posh poshto clear people out of the way. It's in the oases of Xinjiang that you discover the essence of Chinese Central Asia.

At the Bank

account	hisawat
amount	hisawat sommisi
buying rate	setiwelish närgi
cash	näh pul
cashier	kassir
cheque	chäk (pul cheki)
credit card	inawatlik qart
deposit	(amanät) kötäk
exchange rate	almashturush bahasi
exchange	tigishish (almashturush)
foreign currency	chat'ät puli
money exchange	pul almashturush
official rate	hökümät närqi
receipt	hojjät
signature	imza
travellers' cheque	sayahat chäki
withdrawal	qayturuwitish

At the Post Office

The Chinese post office service is fairly dependable even in Xinjiang, and packages sent abroad arrive intact.

I'd like to send ... to (Australia).	män ... (austriliya) gha äwatmäkchi
How much is it?	bu qanchä pul?
How much does this weigh?	uning eghirliqi qanchilik?

address	adress	insurance	bao shien fay
aerogram	ayrugiram	letter	khät
airmail	ayropostta	parcel	khalta
envelope	konwert	post code/	postta numuri/
fax	faks	office	hana

postcard	atkirit ka	surface mail	atlättiki hät
registered mail	zakaz hät	(urgent) telegram	(jiddi)
stamps	marka		telegiram

Telephone

I want to make a phone call to (Canada).	män (canada)gha telefon berimän
What's the number?	telefon numuri qanchä?
The number is ...	telefon numuri ...
Hello.	wäy
Can I speak to ...?	män ... bilan sözläshsäm bolamdu?
collect call	telefon qobul qilghuchi pul räsmi yitimi ätäydigan telefon
country/city code	watan/shähär numuri
directory	telefon (nomuri) däptiri
engaged	(telefon) simi bosh ämäs
international call	halqaraliq telefon
public telephone	omüm ishlitidighan telefon
telephone (number)	telefon (numuri)
wrong number	khata numur

UYGHUR

Sightseeing

What's the name of this place?	bu yerning eti nimä?
Excuse me, what's this/that?	kächürüng, bu/u nimä?
Do you have a (local) map?	sizdä (yärlik) häritä barmu?
Am I allowed to take photos here?	bu yärdä räsim tartsam bolamdu?
What are the opening hours?	saät nächidin?
It's open from (9) to (5).	saät (toqquz)din saät (bäsh)gichi echiludu

How much is the ...?	... qanchä pul?
admission fee	bilät bahasi
guidebook	sayahät qollan misi
postcard	atkiritka

ancient	qädimi	monument	khatirä munarisi
archaeology	arkhilogiyä	museum	moziy
building	bina	old city	qädimi shähär

ruins	harabä(harabiliq)	statues	häykäl
souvenirs	khatirä boyumi	theatres	teaterhana

IN THE COUNTRY

Travelling to many towns and villages requires the permission of Public Security – the government's internal national police force, called 'gong an ju' in Mandarin. This can be organised from the local office.

Travelling through the countryside of Xinjiang can be taxing but the Uyghur people are quite friendly and frequently invite foreign visitors into their homes. Feel comfortable about coaxing your way to attend weekend weddings which are frequent in winter months.

Weather

What's the weather like today/ tomorrow?	bügün/ätä hawarayi qandaq?
The weather's nice today.	bügün hawa yakhshi
Will it rain tomorrow?	ätä yämghur yaghamdu?
It's hot.	issiq
It's raining.	yamghur yeghiwatidu

It's ...	hawa ...
fine	yakhshi
clear/cloudy	ochuq/bulutluq
dark/sunny	qaranghu/nurluq
very cold/hot	bäk soghoq/issiq
snowing	qar
sunrise/sunset	kün chiqish/olturush
windy	shamal

Along the Way

When do we go?	qachan yolgha chiqimiz?
Where are we?	biz qäyärdä?
Can you please tell me how to get to ...?	...-gä qandaq baridighanlighini eytip biralämsiz?
What will we pass on the way?	biz yolda qayärlärdin ötimiz?
How far is it from here to ...?	bu yärdin ...-gä qanchilik ariliq bar?
Is there any thing to see here/there?	bu yärdä körushkä tigishlik nimilar bar?

Let's take a rest here.   bu yärdä däm atoyli.
Can I have a cup of water/tea?   bir istakan su/chay berimu?
What's this/that?   bu/u nimä?

Seasons

spring	bahar (ätäyaz)	autumn	küz
summer	yaz	winter	qish

cave	öngkür	map	kharitä
country	yeza	mountain range	tagh-liq rayun
desert	qumluq	mountain (trail)	tagh (yoli)
earth	yär shari	mudslide	lay ghulishi
farm	yeza igilik	river	därya (östüng)
	mäydani	road	yol
farmer	dikhan	rock	tash
high plateau	igizlik	seasons	pasillar
hill	döng (idir)	valley	jilgha
hot springs	arshang	village	känt
lake	köl	well	quduq
landslide	tagh ghulishi		

Animals

birds	qushlar	monkey	maymun
cat	müshük	pig	chushka
dog	it	rat	chashqan
donkey	ishäq	sheep	qöy
horse	at		

FOOD

In the villages Uyghurs eat while seated on a heatable platform called a kang. Guests will sit around a small short-legged table. At informal settings, they may eat around a standard table and chairs. At large gatherings, like weddings, Uyghurs will sit on carpets on the floor where a cloth is placed marking the eating area. Guests' hands will be washed by the host who pours water out of a pitcher into the guests' hands. Depending on the type of food, Uyghurs usually eat with chopsticks or with their hands. When finished eating, Uyghurs make the same hand motion as made after shaking hands: the hands are placed in front of the face and with an outward circular motion the hands are drawn down in a gesture resembling stroking a beard.

UYGHUR

bar	haraq khana (mai khana)
Chinese restaurant	khänzu resturani
food	tamaq
foodstall	ashkhana
market	bazar
restaurant	resturan
tea house	chay hana
Uyghur food	uyghur tamaqi

At the Restaurant

Can I see the menu please?	tamaq tizimligini körsätkan bolsingiz?
I'll try that.	mäuni tartip bäkay
I'd like what he's eating.	mawu ish yidighan tamaq, män mu alimän
Do you have an English menu?	in'gilischä tamaq tizimligi barmu?
Can you recommend any dishes?	qandaq yakhshi tamaqliringiz bar?
Do you have a knife and fork?	pichaq häm wilkingiz barmu?
The bill please.	hisawat qiling
I don't eat meat.	gösh yimäymän

Breakfast, Lunch & Dinner

I'd like to have ...	män ... alimän
alcoholic drinks	haraq
beverages	ichimlich
lunch/dinner	chüshlük/kächlik tamaq
a snack	qushumchä tamaq
a kebab	kawap

breakfast	ätigänlik tamaq	milk	süt
eggs	tukhum	tea	chay
flat bread	nan		

chüchürä	mutton-filled tortellini in soup
gösh nan	nan bread with mutton
gürüch	rice
langmen	spaghetti-like pulled noodles

manta	steamed dumplings
polo	rice pilaf and mutton
samsa/sambursa	roasted bread pockets with mutton
suyuq ash	mutton soup with noodles
ügrä	noodles

SHOPPING

In the bazaars, bargaining is welcomed, but in department stores the prices are fixed. Don't shake hands with merchants unless you've agreed on the price. It's also important to count your change before leaving the shop.

How many?	nächä?
How much?	qanchä pul?
I'd like to buy ...	män ... almaqchi
I'm just looking.	man päqät köriwatimän
How much does this/that cost?	bu/u qanchä pul?
That's very expensive.	u bäk qimmät ikän
That's cheap.	u qimmät emes
Can you reduce the price?	bahasini biraz chüshürüp biramsiz?
Where can I buy a ...?	män ... ni qayärdin alalay?
Where's the nearest bazaar?	äng yeqindiki bazaar qayärdä?

UYGHUR

Sizes & Quantities

a bottle/container of	bir sisä
dozen	on ikki
half a dozen	altä
one metre/litre	bir metir/litir
two kilometres	ikki kilometir

Colours

black	qara	light brown	uch kongur
blue	kök	red	kizil
brown	kongur	white	aq
green	yeshil	yellow	sarik
grey	kul		

UYGHUR

HEALTH

There are three types of medicine available in Xinjiang: western, Chinese and Uyghur. Uyghur medicine, unani tibbi, is based on ancient Greek and Ayurvedic medicine from India. Uyghur and Chinese medicines are slower acting than western. For minor stomach ailments, try the Uyghur miracle drug called gül kän, which is made of fermented crushed rose petals. For a major illness, try to get to an international clinic in Beijing. While most doctors are competent and trained locally, there is a tendency to be cautious and to hospitalise foreigners. Get second and third opinions before being treated especially if the diagnosis seems bizarre. Common colds can be diagnosed as early stages of pneumonia, tooth pain can provoke recommendations for tooth extraction. Remember that you have the right to refuse care.

I'm sick.	män kisäl (mining mijäzim yoq)
My friend is sick.	aghimäm kisäl
I need a doctor.	man dokhturgha körinimän
I need a doctor who can speak English.	manga in'gilischa sözliyäläydighan dokhtur kiräk
I want a doctor who practises western medicine.	mangä gharpshä dawaliyalaydighan dokhtur kiräk
Can you bring a doctor to my room?	yatighimgha bir dokhtur bashlap külsingiz?
Please take me to a doctor.	mini dokhturgha elip barsingiz
I've been injured.	män yarilandim
I need an ambulance.	manga jiddi qutquzush masinisi keräk
Can you tell me where the ... is?	manga ... qayärdä ikänligini eytip birälämsiz?
clinic	dawalash bölimi
doctor	dokhtur
hospital	dokhturhana
nurse	sestira
pharmacy	dorahana
I need an English interpreter.	manga bir in'gilischa tärjiman kiräk

I want a female doctor. — manga bir ayal dokhtur kiräk
Please use a new syringe. — yengi ishpiris ishlätsingiz
I have my own syringe. — özäm ishpirisi bar
I don't want a blood transfusion. — män qan saldur maymän
I'm not feeling well. — mijazim yoq
How long before it will get better? — yakhshi bolup kitishkä qanchilik waqit kitidu?

THE DOCTOR MAY SAY ...

nimä boldi?	What's wrong?
qayäringiz aghriwatidu?	Where does it hurt?
qandaqraq?	How are you feeling?
aghriwatamdu?	Do you feel any pain?
qizitiwatamsiz?	Do you have a temperature?
burun qandaq kisällar bolghan?	What illness have you had in the past?
tamaka chikämsiz?	Do you smoke?
haraq ichämsiz?	Do you drink?
hamildarmusiz?	Are you pregnant?
künigä(bir) taldin (töt) qetim	Take (1) tablet (4) times a day.
yallughlanaghan yärgä kuniga (ikki) qetim sürüsh	Apply to the affected area (twice) a day.
tamaqtin burun/kiyin	before/after meal
uhlashtin burun	before bedtime

UYGHUR

Parts of the Body

arm	biläk	kidney	böräk
bone	ustihan	leg	pachaq
ear	qulaq	liver	jigür
eye	köz	lung	öpkä
face	yüz	mouth	eghiz
finger	barmaq	muscle	muskule
foot	put	pulse	qan tumuri
hand	qol	skin	tirä
head	bash (kalla)	stomach	ashqazan
heart	yüräk	urine	süydük

UYGHUR

Ailments

I ...	män ...
have an insect bite	mini hasharät kheqiwaldi
can't sleep	uhliyalmayman
have a heart condition	yuräk hastali bar
lost my appetite	ishtiyim yoq
have missed my period for ... months	... ay isimni yoqutup qoydum
have a high pulse rate	tomurum ittik soyup kitip baridu
am pregnant	hamildur
vomited	qusuwättim
am weak	ajiz
can't move my ...	... qimirlitalmayman

I have ...	man ... bar
altitude sickness	igizlik qorqush kisiliy ägirip
asthma	astmam
diabetes	qant siyish kisili
diarrhoea	ich sürüsh kisili
dizziness	bash qaymaq
a fever	qizitma
hepatitis	jigär kisili
an itch	yäl
lice	pit
a migraine	tutup-tutup bash aghrish
a pain	aghrimaq
a stomachache	qorsaq aghriqi
venereal disease	jinsiy kisällik

I'm allergic to (antibiotics).	män (antibiotiklar/baktiriyägä qarshi) bilän yallughlandim

At the Chemist

Do you have ...?	(manga) ... barmu?
aspirin	aspirin
Band-Aids	hamildarliqtin saqilinish naychisi
condom	biyun tao (prezervativ)
cough remedy	zukam dorisi

eyedrops	köz dorisi
painkiller	aghriq tokhtutushi dorisi
sanitary napkins	ay körüsh weishengjin
sleeping pill	timichlandurush dorisi
contraceptive pills	hamildarliqtin saqlinish dorisi
travel sickness pill	sayahät kisili dorisi

At the Dentist

dentist	chish dokhturi
tooth/teeth	chish/chishlar
toothache	chish aghriqi
wisdom tooth	äqil chishi
Is there a dentist here?	bu yärdächish dokhturi barmu?
I don't want it extracted.	män chishimni tartquz mayman
Please give me an anaesthetic.	mini kushsizlandurup qoyung

Useful Words

accident	hadis
acupuncture	yingnäsanchish
AIDS	aysi bing
antibiotic	antibiotik
antiseptic	chirishkä turidighan qarshi
blood	qan chiqish
blood group/test	qan tipi/täkshürüsh
contraceptive	hamildarliqning aldini
eye (drops)	köz (-üchün dora)
first aid	jiddi qutquzush
glasses	közäynäk
injection	ukul urush
menstruation	ay körüsh
optometrist	köz äynäk salghuchi
pneumonia	öpkäyallughi
Red Cross	qizil kirisit
specialist	käspi dokhtur
surgeon	tashqi kisälliklar dokhturi
syringe	ishpiris
virus	virus
vitamin	vitamin
X-ray	rentigin nuri

TIME, DATES & FESTIVALS
Telling the Time

When?	qachan?
What time is it?	saät qanchä boldi?

hour	saät
... o'clock	saät ...
half past ...	... yerim
a quarter (15 minutes)	charäk (on bäsh minut)
morning	ätigän
afternoon	chüshtin kiyin
noon	chüsh
evening	käch
midnight	yerim kechä

Days of the Week

Saturday	shänbä	Wednesday	charshänbä
Sunday	yäkshänbä	Thursday	päyshänbä
Monday	düshänbä	Friday	jümä
Tuesday	sayshänbä		

Months

January	yanwar	July	iyul
February	fewral	August	awghust
March	mart	September	sentäbr
April	aprel	October	öktäbir
May	may	November	noyabir
June	iyun	December	dekabir

The Muslim Calendar

The Islamic calendar is lunar unlike the longer western solar calendar.

muharamul haram	rajabul murajab
safarul muzafar	shuban-ul-mazem
rabi-ul-awal	ramazan-ul-mubarak
rabi-ul-Sani	shawal-ul-mukaram
jamadi-ul-awal	ze qaidatul haram
jamadi-ul-akher	ze hejatul haram

UYGHUR

Present, Past & Future

today	bügün	last week	ötkän häptä
yesterday	tünügün	next week	kelär häptä
tomorrow	ätä	this month	bu ay
tonight	akhsham	last month	ötkän ay
tomorrow evening	ätäkichä	next month	kelär yil
(this) week	(bu) häptä		

Festivals & Holidays

Twelfth of rabi-ul-awal – Birth of Prophet Mohammad (P.B.U.H.)

First of shawal – roza heyt (eid-ul-fitr) marking the end of the ramadan-ul-mubarak Islamic fast

Tenth of zil hejja – qurban heyt (eid-ul-adha, eid uz-zuha) Three day Islamic festival commemorating Ibrahim's (Abraham's) attempted sacrifice of his son (Ismail according to Islam, Isaac according to Judaism) whereby God intervenes providing a sheep for sacrifice instead of the child. It's during this festival that Muslims make their hajj to Mecca. Muslims sacrifice livestock and feast in celebration.

March 21 – näwroz bayrimi a New Year festival celebrated by Persian speaking and nomadic Turkic peoples of Central Asia but growing to be celebrated by most Central Asians both sedentary and nomadic.

October 1 – dölät bayrimi (Chinese National Day)

UYGHUR

NUMBERS

0	nöl	11	on bir	22	yigirmä ikki
1	bir	12	on ikki	23	yigirmä üch
2	ikki	13	on üch	30	ottuz
3	üch	14	on töt	39	ottuz toqquz
4	töt	15	on bäsh	40	qiriq
5	bäsh	16	on altä	50	ällik
6	altä	17	on yättä	60	atmish
7	yättä	18	on säkkiz	70	yätmish
8	säkkiz	19	on toqquz	80	säksän
9	toqquz	20	yigirmä	90	toqsan
10	on	21	yigirmä bir	100	bir yüz

UYGHUR

101	bir yüz bir	1001	bir ming bir
110	bir yüz on	10,000	on ming
115	bir yüz on bäsh	100,000	bir yüz ming
120	bir yüz yigirmä	one million	bir milyon
190	bir yüz toqsan	10 million	on milyon
200	ikki yüz	100 million	yüz milyon
1000	bir ming	one billion	bir milyard

EMERGENCIES

Help!	yardämgä!
Danger!	hatarlik!
Don't move!	midermang!
Stop.	tokhtung
Go away.	keting
Listen, we're not interested.	anlang, biz buni qiziqmaymiz
Call the police.	saqchilar chakiring
Call a doctor.	doktor chakiring
Call an ambulance immediately.	tez qutquzush mashinasi chakiringlar
Could you help me please?	mangga yardäm beralämsiz?
There's been an accident.	hadisi chikip boldi.
I've been injured.	män yarilandim
I've been raped.	bir adam mangga changjian kildi
I've been robbed.	bir aldamchi mening närsilär alawetti
Could I please use the telephone?	telefon islitish bolamdu?
I wish to contact my embassy.	özämning elchihananigha gäp berishim kiräk

Uzbek

UZBEK

INTRODUCTION

Uzbek is a direct descendent of the Turkic literary language that developed in the 13th and 14th centuries. It's spoken by nearly 20 million people scattered in 11 countries. The speakers in Uzbekistan (more than 15 million) are found in its cities like the capital Tashkent and the ancient fabled cities of Bukhara, Samarkand and Khiva, and in the volatile Ferghana Valley. Uzbek is also spoken by 1.5 million in Afghanistan; 1.3 million in Tajikistan; 575,000 in Kyrgyzstan; 350,000 in Kazakhstan; 330,000 in Turkmenistan; 130,000 in Russia; over 20,000 in each of Ukraine, the USA and Mongolia; and 16,000 in China.

PRONUNCIATION

The Uzbek language is written in the Cyrillic script in Uzbekistan and in a modified Persian-Arabic script in China. Both the Chinese and Soviet governments imposed the changes to a Cyrillic and Roman script with the hopes of breaking the Uzbeks' ties to the Muslim world. After Uzbekistan independence, many countries have pushed the government to change their script. Turkey has pushed a Roman script and Muslim countries have lobbied for an Arabic script. The transliteration system used in this phrasebook for all languages is an attempt to unify the Central Asian languages around a system that uses Roman letters.

Most Uzbek sounds are also found in the English language, while a few additional ones must be learned. Intonation is important and this can be learned quickly by listening to Uzbeks speak. The Uyghur and Uzbek languages are so close that those who use Uyghur to speak to Uzbeks will likely be asked why they are speaking Uzbek with a Uyghur accent.

Vowels

There are seven vowels in the Uzbek language and almost all correspond to English sounds, except the sound ö which is produced with rounded lips.

Uzbek Language Area

0   250   500 km

The external boundaries of India on this map have not been authenticated and may be correct

KAZAKHSTAN
UZBEKISTAN KYRGYZSTAN
TURKMENISTAN TAJIKISTAN CHINA
AFGHANISTAN
IRAN
PAKISTAN
INDIA

RUSSIA

Aqtöbe ●

✪ Astana   ● Semey

● Karaganda

KAZAKHSTAN

Lake Balkash

Aral Sea   ● Kizilorda   ● Yining

Moynaq ●   ● Almaty

Nukus ●   Taraz ●   ✪ Bishkek

UZBEKISTAN   Shymkent ● KYRGYZSTAN

Tashkent ✪   Andijan
● Osh

Bukhara ●   Samarkand ●   ● Kashgar   CHINA
(Xinjiang)

TAJIKISTAN
TURKMENISTAN   ✪ Dushanbe

✪ Ashghabat
● Mary

Mazar-i-Sharif ●   PAKISTAN   CHINA
(Tibet)
IRAN   ✪ Kabul
● Herat   INDIA
AFGHANISTAN

UZBEK

a	as in 'father'	o	as in 'go'
e	as in 'bet'	ö	as the 'e' in 'her' pronounced
ë	as the 'ÿe' in 'yet'		with well-rounded lips
i	as in 'bill'	u	as in 'put'

Consonants

h	with aspiration as in 'haste'
j	as in 'jar'
p	slightly muffled as in 'push'
q	a hard 'k' as in the Arab country 'Qatar'
r	slightly trilled, soft, and close to an 'l' sound

The consonants written with two letters (cluster) are fairly easy to learn. The ch and sh are found in English. The four other clusters will take practise but if they are too difficult in the beginning you can pronounce the gh as an 'r', the kh as an 'h', and zh like a 'j' and you'll eventually be understood.

ch	as in 'cheek'
gh	similar to the French 'r' (see page 16 for an explanation)
kh	a slightly guttural sound like the 'ch' in the Scottish 'loch'
ng	as the 'ng' in 'rung'
sh	as the 'sh' in 'sheep'
zh	like the 's' in 'vision' and 'treasure'

GREETINGS & CIVILITIES

There are different forms of greetings for men and women. The polite form of greeting for men is holding the left hand on the chest near the heart. By that, men express respect and sympathy to the other man.

Women usually don't shake hands with other women nor with men. Women touch each other's shoulders with their right hand and slightly stroke them. Women kiss each other on the cheeks three times (two on one cheek and one on the other) if they have not seen each other for a long time or if they are very close relatives or friends.

UZBEK

Please.	marhamat
Please sit down.	marhamat otiring
Thank you.	rahmat
Excuse/Pardon me.	kechirasiz
Never mind.	ha bopti (qöyabering)
Correct.	töghri
Good.	yakhshi
OK.	zör/nishtak
Do you understand?	tushunyapsizmi?
No.	yöq
Yes.	ha
I understand.	men tushunyapman
I don't understand.	men tushunmayapman
Sorry.	uzr
No problem.	hech qisi yöq
Please wait awhile.	iltimos ozgina sabr qiling
Where's the toilet?	hojatkhona qaerda?

Greetings & Goodbyes

The greeting salomaleikum and the reply valeikum-assalom can be used for all occasions. The phrases hair and salomat boling are appropriate conversation endings for all occasions.

Good morning/day/evening.	salomaleikum (lit: peace be upon you)
And upon you peace.	tinch böling
Good night.	hairli tun
How are you?	qandaisiz?
I'm fine.	men zörman
Fine (and you)?	zör (özingizchi)?
Not bad.	yomon emas
How's your health?	soghlghingiz qandai/qanaqa/qalai?
Have you eaten?	ovqatlandingizmi/tamadduq/ qildingizmi?
Where are you going?	qaerga ketyapsiz
What are you doing?	nima qilyapsiz?
Goodbye.	hair
See you tomorrow.	ërtagacha hair

UZBEK

Have a good trip.	safaringiz behatar bölsin
May your travels be free of obstacles.	yöl bolsin
See you soon.	körishguncha hair
You've been a great help.	siz katta yordam körsatdingiz

LANGUAGE DIFFICULTIES

Do you speak English?	siz inglizcha gaplashasizmi?
I don't speak English.	men inglizcha gaplasha olmaiman
I don't speak Uzbek/Russian.	men uzbekchada/ruscha gaplasha olmaiman
Do you have an interpreter?	tarjimoningiz bormi?
How do you say that in Uzbek?	uzbekchada buni qandai talaffuz qilasiz?
Can you repeat that please?	iltimos qaitara olmaisizmi?
Could you speak louder/ slower please?	iltimos balandroq/sekinroq gapira olmaisizmi?
Please point to the phrase in the book.	iltimos kitobdagi jumlani körsating
Just a minute.	ozgina sabr qiling
What does it mean?	buning ma'nosi nima?

SMALL TALK
Meeting People

People nod to one another when a friend or relative is at a considerable distance away, or when a person is in a hurry. If people meet someone who is just an acquaintance or not a close relative, they may only nod to each other. It's very polite and normal to ask about the health of one's parents and family.

Who are you looking for?	kimni akhtarayapsiz?
Yes, he's here.	ha, u shu erda

No, he's not here. yöq, u bu erda ëmas
What's your name? sizning ismingiz nima?
What's your father's name? otangizning ismi nima?
Who are you? siz kimsiz?
I'm pleased to meet you. sizni uchratganimdan
  hursandman

So am I. men ham
What time is it? soat necha böldi?
What's this? bu nima?
Are your parents alive? ota onangiz hayotmilar?
My (mother) is alive but my mening (onam) hayot lekin
(father) is not. (otam) olamdan ötgan

Nationalities

Common questions that Uzbeks ask travellers are the country where
they are from, their name, and the purpose of their visit.

What country are you from? qaisi mamlakatdan keldingiz?
What ethnic group are you from? millatingiz nima?
I come from (the USA). men (amerikadan) keldim

Age

How old are you? yoshingiz nechada?
How old do you think I am? meni yoshim nechada deb
  öilaisiz?
I think you are (35) years old. menimcha sizning yoshingiz
  (öttiz besh)da

Religion

What religion do you believe in? qaisi dinga ishonasiz?

I'm (a) ... men ... ishonaman
  Buddhist budda diniga
  Catholic katolik diniga
  Christian hristian diniga
  Confucianism konfutsiilikga
  Hindu hindu diniga
  Jewish yahudii diniga
  Muslim islom diniga

UZBEK

I'm not religious.	men dindor ëmasman
Do you attend Mosque?	machitga borib turaiszmi?
I attend Mosque every Friday.	men machitga har juma kuni borib turaman

Clicking accompanied by shaking the head may signify disapproval. Just clicking means surprise or bitterness. It should be noted that it isn't polite to make a lot of sounds or use gestures among elderly or respected people. When people apologise they don't look in the eyes of the other person. They look at the ground with their left hand on their chest at the area of the heart.

Family

This is my ...	bu mening ...
father	öam/adam/dadam
mother	onam/oyim
husband/wife	ërim/hotinim
girlfriend/boyfriend	yigitim/qizim
son/daughter	öghlim/qizim
younger brother/sister	ukam/singlim
older brother/sister	akam/opam

Are you married?	turmush qurganmisiz?
I'm married.	turmush qurganman
I'm single.	böydoqman (m)/turmush qurmaganman (f)

How many children do you have?	nechta farzandingiz bor?
I don't have any children.	mening farzandim yöq
How many brothers/sisters do you have?	nechta akanlaringiz/ singllaringizingiz bor?
I don't have any brothers/ sisters.	mening bironta akam/ singlim yöq

UZBEK

GETTING AROUND

I'd like to go to ...	men ...ga borishni istaiman
How can I get to ...?	men qandai qilib ... ga bora olaman?
Which (bus) do I take to get to ...?	... ga borish uchun qaisi (abtobusga) chiqishim zarur?
Is there another way to get there?	u erga borishni boshqa yoli bormi?
What time does the next ... leave/arrive?	keingi ... soat nechada keladi/ketadi?
bus	abtobus
train	poezd
plane	taiyora/samolet
Where's the ...?	... qaerda?
airport	taiyoragoh/aeroport
bus stop	avtobus bekati
bus terminal	avtobus sönggi bekati
train station	poezd bekati
ticket office	patta (bilet)kassasi
Is it far?	bu uzoqdami?
Yes, it's far.	ha uzoqda
It's quite close.	yaqingina
Can I walk there?	u erga piyoda borsam buladimi?
How much time will it take to walk there?	u erga piyoda borsam qancha vaqt ketadi?
What's the address?	u erning manzilgohi (adresi) nima?
Please write down the address for me.	iltimos manzilgohni (adresni) men uchun yozib bering
Could you tell the taxi driver the address please?	iltimos haidovchiga manzilni(adresni) aita olasizmi?
Please draw a map for me.	iltimos men uchun harita chizib bering

UZBEK

Directions

Directions are normally given by pointing with the index finger toward the place or object. When indicating somewhere a long distance away, Uzbeks speak with high pitched voices.

Which direction?	qaisi tomonga?
Go straight ahead.	töghriga yuring
Turn left/right.	chapga/öngga qairiling
north/south	shimol/janub
east/west	shraq/gharb
southeast/northwest	janubi–sharq/shimoli–gharb
uphill/downhill	tepalik/pastlik
left/right	chap/öng
at the corner	burchakda
up/down	tepa/past (quii)
upstairs/downstairs	tepada/pastda
far away	uzoqda
inside/outside	ichkari/tashqari
middle	örta
near (to ...)	(... ga) yaqin
that direction	ana bu tomon
this direction	bu tomon

Buying Tickets

Where's the ticket office?	pattalar(biletlar) qaerda sotiladi?
I would like a (1st class) ticket to (Tashkent).	menga (tashkent)gacha (birinchi toifa) pattasi kerak
How much is the train to (Samarkand)?	(samarkand)gacha poezd pattasi (bileti) qancha turadi?
Is there a ticket for the bus to (Bukhara) today?	bugun (bukhara)ga boradigan avtobus uchun patta (bilet) bormi?
What is the cheapest fare to Tashkent?	(tashkent)-gacha ëng arzon patta qancha turadi?
There are no tickets.	pattalar yöq
berth number	tokchalik/polkalik kupe
berth upper/lower	tokcha/polka yuqori/quii

cancelled	bekor qilingan
confirm	tasdiqlamoq
dormitory bunk	yotoqhona
first/second/economy class	birinchi/ikkinchi/iqtisodiy toifa
one-way ticket	bir tamonga patta
return tickets	patta qaitarish
refund	badal
seat	örin
student's ticket	talaba pattasi (bileti)
ticket office	patta kassasi
timetable	jadval

Air

Airports are dangerous in terms of crime. It's very difficult to get information about anything. Checked-in luggage is handled by the airport workers carelessly, and after arrival you should hurry to get your luggage, otherwise it may disappear forever.

| I want to confirm my flight. | men özimning uchishimni tasdiqlamoqchiman |
| This price is higher than normal. | bu narkh odatdagidan baland |

aeroplane	tayora (samolet)
airline ticket	tayora (samolet) uchun patta
customs' (declaration)	boj (deklaratsiasi)
departure	parvoz
estimated time of arrival/ departure	manzilga etishning/parvoz boshlanishing tahminiy vaqti
gate number	darvoza raqami
no smoking	chekilmasin
passport	pasport

Bus

Is this going to the (bazaar)?	bu (bozorga) boradimi?
I want to get off at ...	men ... da tushib qolishni istaiman
Please tell me when we've reached that stop.	iltimos, haligi bekatga etganimizda menga ma'lum qiling

| bus (terminal) | avtobus (sönggi bekati) |
| long-distance bus station | sharlararo qatnöv avtobus bekati |

Train

Trains are noisy and not very comfortable. They don't have air conditioning, are usually pretty dirty and frequently late.

Can you help me find my seat/berth please?	menga joyimni/honamni topishga yordam bera olmaisizmi?
Excuse me, this is my seat.	kechirasiz, bu mening joyim
Where's the dining car?	vagon–restoran qaerda?

dining car	vagon–restoran
(express) fast train	(express) tezkor poezd
hard seat (2nd class)	ikkinchi toifa örni (platskartniy)
hard-sleeper (2nd class)	ikkinchi toifa kupesi
soft-seat (1st class)	birinchi (klas) toifa
train	poezd

Taxi

Signalling with your hand is usually enough to stop a taxi. Not all of them have meters, so to negotiate you should know the rate per kilometre set by the government and a rough idea of how far you're going. Tipping isn't common but the drivers appreciate it very much. Men usually sit in the front seat while women take the back seats.

I would like to go to ...	men ... ga borishni istaiman
How long does it take to go to ...?	... ga borish uchun qancha vaqt ketadi?
Are any English speaking drivers available?	inglizchada gapiradigan haidovchilar bormi?
How much?	qancha?
Please stop here.	shu erda tökhtang
Stop at the next corner.	keyingi muyulishda tökhtang
Please hurry/slow down.	iltimos tezroq/sekinroq
Please wait here.	iltimos shu erda kutib turing
I'll get off here.	men shu erda tushib qolaman
Where can I hire a taxi?	qaerda taxi topishim mumkin?

UZBEK

How much is it for one/ three day(s)

bir/uch kun gacha qancha böladi?

Useful Words

accident	bahtsiz hodisa	(international)	(halqaro)
battery	batareya	driving	haidovchi
bicycle	velosiped	licence	guvohnomasi
brake	tormoz	map	harita
car	engil	motorbike	mototsikl
	avtomobil	parking	töhtash joii
engine oil	motor moyi	petrol	benzin
fill up	tölidirish	radiator	radiator
flat tyre	puchqaigan	service station	avto service
	ghildirak	taxi stand	taxi bekati
headlight	oldingi fara	towing a car	shatakga olish
highway	shoh köcha	tyre	ghildirak

ACCOMMODATION

hotel/inn	mehmonhona
apartment	honadon
dormitory	yotoqhona
guesthouse	mehmonlar uii
youth hostel	yoshlar yotoqhonasi
campsite	lager joii

Where's a guesthouse?	mehmonlar uii qaerda?
I'd like to book a room.	men hona buyurtma qilmoqchiman

I'm looking for a ... hotel.

men ... mehmonhonasini ahtarayapman

cheap	arzon
clean	toza
good	yakhshi
near-the-city	shaharga yaqin
near-the-airport	tayoragohga yaqin
nearby	yaqin orada

UZBEK

The number of hotels is increasing tremendously. They range from one to four-star hotels and the rates are not negotiable. Some provide a significant number of services and are very clean.

It's also possible to stay with families. If it isn't a purely commercial arrangement, it's better to present a gift rather than paying cash. Food, some clothing, and accessories could be good gifts.

Booking a Room

Do you have any rooms/beds?	bösh honangiz/kravatlaringiz bormi?
I'd like a ...	men ... hohlaiman
single room	alohida hona
quiet room	tinch hona
twin room	ikkita honalik nomer
big room	katta hona
(double) bed	(ikki kishilik) kravat

At the Hotel

How much is it per night/person?	bir kecha/kishi uchun qancha tölanadi?
Is there a discount for students/children?	talaba/yosh bolalar uchun chegirtmalar bormi?
Can I get a discount if I stay longer?	men uzoqroq tursam chegirtma berasizmi?
Are there any cheaper ones?	arzonroqlari bormi?
Can I see the room first?	avval honani körsam böladimi?
Are there any others?	boshqalari bormi?
I like this/that room.	men bu/shu honani yoqtiryapman
It's fine, I'll take this room.	bunisi yakhshi, men bu honada turaman
I'm going to stay for ...	men ... turmoqchiman
one/two night(s)	bir/ikki kecha
a few days	bir necha kun
a week	bir hafta
Can I have the key please?	iltimos, menga kalitni bering?
Is hot water available all day?	issiq suv kun böi bormi?

Could I have a different room?	menga boshqa hona bormi?
Any messages for me?	men uchun hech qandai habar yöqmi?
Please do not disturb.	iltimos bezovta qilmang

Requests & Complaints

It's too ...	bu juda ...
big/small	katta/kichkina
hot/cold	issiq/sovuq
dark/dirty	qaronghi/iflos
noisy	shovqun-suron

It smells.	bundan yomon hid kelyapti
The toilet/sink is blocked.	tualet/rakovina tölib qolgan
The door is locked.	ëshik qulflangan
My room number is (123).	mening honamning raqami (bir yuz yigirma uch)

| Please fix it as soon as possible. | iltimos buni iloji boricha tezroq tuzating |

Checking Out

I'd like to check out now/ tomorrow.	men hozir/ërtaga köchib ketmoqchiman
I'd like to pay the bill.	men hisobni tölamoqchiman
Can I leave my luggage here for a few days?	men özimning yukimni/bagazhimni shu erda tashlab kemoqchiman
Thank you for your hospitality.	mehmondorchiligingiz uchun rahmat

I'm returning ...	men ... qaityapman
tomorrow	ërtaga
in 2-3 days	ikki–uch kundan söng
next week	keiingi hafta

Useful Words

address	manzilgoh	bathroom	hojathona
baggage	yuk (bagazh)	bed	kravat
balcony	balkon	bill	hisob
basin	bassein	blanket	korpa (odeyalo)

UZBEK

bucket	paqir	luggage	yuk (bagazh)
caretaker	yordamchi	reception desk	qabul stoli
key	kalit	room	hona
light bulb	chiroq	shower	hammomhona
lobby	dahliz	sleeping bag	uiqu qopi
lock	qulf	toilet	tualet

AROUND TOWN

Towns look crowded because of the large number of pedestrians, but most are fairly clean. Russians, Russian-speakers and the majority of Uzbek youth dress in western style. Elderly Uzbeks and Central Asians dress in national robes chopon and caps duppi

At the Bank

account	hisob
amount	miqdor
buying rate	sotib olish tarifi
cash	naqd pul
cheque	chek
credit card	kredit kartochkasi
deposit	bank hisobi
exchange rate	airbosh kursi
foreign currency	chet ël valyutasi
official rate	rasmiy kurs
receipt	ma'lumot noma (spravka)
signature	qöl
travellers' cheque	sayohatchilar cheki
withdrawal	bankdagi hisobdan pul olish

At the Post Office

The quality of the postal service isn't very good. Sometimes you have to wait a long time to get service. Except for Russian, knowledge of a foreign language is not very common.

I'd like to send ... to (Australia).	men ... ni (avstraliyaga) yuborishni istaiman
How much is it?	buning narkhi qancha?
How much does this weigh?	buning vazni qancha?

UZBEK

surface mail	er yuzi transporti orqali yuborilgan hat
address	manzilgoh/adres
aerogram	aerogram
airmail	avia pochtasi
envelope	konvert
fax	faks
letter	hat
parcel	posilka
postcard	gulqoghoz
post code	pochta indexi
poste restante	talabga binoan (do vostrebovania)
post office	aloqa bölimi
registered mail	buyurtma hati
stamps	markalar
(urgent) telegram	(tezkor) telegramma

Telephone

I want to make a long-distance call to (London).	men (london)ga qönghiroq qilishni istaiman
What's the number?	raqami necha?
The number is ...	raqami ...
Hello.	salom
Can I speak to ...?	... gaplashsam böladimi?

collect call	özga shahs hisobiga qonghiroq
country code	mamlakat kodi
directory	telefon kitobchasi
engaged	band
international call	halqaro qönghiroq
public telephone	köcha telefoni
telephone (number)	telefon (raqami)
wrong number	notoghri raqam

UZBEK

Sightseeing

Most people don't mind having their photo taken. In the evenings, there are bars and restaurants to go to, and a lot of wedding parties where everyone's welcome. Uzbeks say ailanib kelalilik, or 'Let's go and look around'.

What's the name of this place?	bu erning nomi nima?
Excuse me, what's this/that?	kechirasiz bu/shu nima?
Do you have a local map?	sizda bu erninig haritasi yoqmi?
Am I allowed to take photos here?	bu erda rasmga olish ruhsat étilganmi?
What time does it open/close?	bu soat nechada ochiladi/ yopiladi?

How much is the ...?	... qancha
admission fee	kirish haqqi
guidebook	yöllovchi kitob
postcard	gulqoghoz (otkritka)

ancient	qadimiy	ruins	harobalar
archaeology	arheologiya	sculpture	haikal
building	bino	sightseeing	ékskursiya
monument	monument	souvenirs	ésdaliklar
museum	saroy	statues	haikallar
old city	éski shahar	theatres	teatrlar

IN THE COUNTRY

Getting to outlying villages is very difficult and you have to wait a long time for a bus. In the countryside there are a lot of dogs, cats, cows, horses, sheep and chickens. Sometimes you can run into snakes, scorpions and reptiles. There are also a lot of cotton plants, mint grass, apple, peach, pear and apricot trees.

Weather

What is the weather like today/ tomorrow?	bugun/értaga obhavo qandai böladi?
The weather's nice today.	bugun obhavo yakhshi
Will it rain tomorrow?	értaga yomghir yoghadimi?
It is hot.	issiq
It's raining.	yomghir yoghayapti

It's ...	
fine/bright	a'lo/yoriq
clear/cloudy	ochiq/bulutli
dark/sunny	qaronghi/quyoshli

UZBEK

| very cold/hot | juda sovuq/issiq |
| very windy/wet | juda shabada/höl |

flood	toshqin		sunrise	quyosh chiqishi
fog	tuman		sunset	quyosh botishi
lightning	chaqmoq		thunder	mömaqaldiroq
rain	yomghir		weather	obhavo
snow	qor		wind	shamol

Along the Way

You can experience a variety of problems on the road: potholes, slow downs for funeral processions, breakdowns, livestock crossing the road and blockades of the street for repair. Sometimes there are thieves who pretend to be passengers but rob the driver and steal the car.

When do we go?	qachon ketamiz?
Where are we?	qaerdamiz?
Can you please tell me how to get to ...?	iltimos menga ...ga qandai etib borishni aita olasizmi?
What will we pass on the way?	yölimizda qaerdan ötamiz?
How far is it from here to ...?	bu erdan ... gacha qanchalik uzoq?
I'd like to look around the village.	qishloghingizni ailanmoqchiman
Are there any things to see here/there?	u erda/shu erda körishga arziydigan narsalar bormi?
Let's take a rest here.	u erda dam olailik?
Can I have a cup of water/tea?	bir piyola suv/choi bera olasizmi?

Seasons

spring	bahor		winter	qish
summer	yoz		seasons	fasllar
autumn	kuz			

Useful Words

cave	ghor		desert	chöl
country	qishloq		earth	er

UZBEK

farm	kolkhoz	mountain	togh (zanjiri/
farmer	dehqon	(range/trail)	yölakchasi)
high plateau	yuqori plato	mudslide	toshqin
hill	tepalik	river	daryo
hot springs	issiq buloq	road	yöl
lake	köl	rock	harsang tosh
landslide	toshqin	valley	vodiy
map	harita	village	qishloq
mountain	togh	well	quduq

Animals & Birds

cat	mushuk	parrot	tötiqush
dog	it	pigeon	kabutar
donkey	ёshak	rat	kalamush
horse	ot	sheep	qöi
monkey	maimun		

UZBEK

FOOD

Traditionally, there are no chairs for the tables, hontahtq which are short-legged and low. People sit on a material called kurpachq similar to mattresses. Legs are placed in different positions, the most common is called chordana– legs are crossed in a way similar to the lotus position. The guests are seated at the head of the table, the father of the host family occupies the best seat available after the guest's seat.

Polq manti, and honum(see below) are eaten with the right hand, while other foods are eaten with forks and spoons.

Bread and hot tea are served first. There are often sweets on the table, but those are more for decoration than for immediate consumption. Substantial food is then served followed by fruits or dessert.

There are plenty of bazaars in each city, and the quality of groceries and their freshness is considerably better than in grocery stores.

food stall	oziq-ovqat rastasi
market	bozor
bar	bar
Afghan/Chinese restaurant	ofghon/hitoi restorani
tea house	choihona
restaurant	restoran

At the Restaurant

Can I see the menu please?	menuni körsam böladimi?
I'll try that.	men buni tatib köraman
I'd like what he's eating.	men u tamaddiq qilayotgan taomndan hohlaiman
Do you have an English menu?	sizda inglizcha menu bormi?
Can you recommend any dishes?	taomlardan birini tavsiya ëta olasizmi?
Do you have a knife and fork?	sizda pichoq va vilka bormi?
The bill please.	iltimos hisobni bering
I don't eat meat.	men gösht emaiman
I'd like to have ...	men ... istaiman
pilaf	palov
food	taomlar
(alcoholic) drinks	(spirtly) ichimliklar

UZBEK

manti	flour, lamb, onion
chuchvara	flour, lamb, onion, potato, water
polo	rice, meat, carrot, onion, chick peas, oil, garlic, raisin
kabob	meat, onion
surva	meat, potato, carrot, onion, tomato, oil, water
jarkop	meat, potato, oil, carrot, onion, garlic
honum	flour, tomato, meat, onion
moshkichiri	rice, meat, oil, onion, tomato, carrot

Breakfast, Lunch & Dinner

For breakfast, people usually eat qaimoq (similar in texture to sour cream or mayonnaise) spread on a piece of bread.

| breakfast | nonushta | dinner | kechqurungi taom |
| lunch | tushlik | snack | engil emak |

bread	non	rice	guruch
eggs	tuhum	tea	choi
milk	sut	yoghurt	qatiq
noodles	laghmon		

bulochka bilan qòi gòshti	buns with mutton
chechevitsa va sabzavotlar	lentils and vegetables
kima	kima
palov va sabzavotlar	rice pilaf and vegetables
qòi gòshti shörvasi	mutton soup with noodle flakes
yopgan non va kabob	roti bread and kebab

SHOPPING

You should stay away from merchants who demand money before they show you their goods. A lot of merchants suggest you try their products free of charge, to check their quality. Some serve tea and tell stories. A handshake means that a deal is made and it's considered a cowardly action to change your mind and walk away after a handshake.

How many?	nechta?
How much?	qancha?
I'd like to buy ...	men ... sotib olishni istaiman

I'm just looking.	men tamosha qilyapman
How much does this/that cost?	bu/ana bu qancha turadi?
That's very expensive.	bu juda qimmat
That's cheap.	bu qimmat ëmas
Can you reduce the price?	narhini tushura olmaisizmi?
Where can I buy a ...?	men qaerda ... ni sotib olishim mumkin?
Where's the nearest bazaar?	ëng yaqin bozor qaerda?

Sizes & Quantities

a bottle/container of	bir butilka/idish
dozen	ön ikki
half a dozen	olti
one metre/litre/kilometre	bir metr/litr/kilometer

Colours

black	qora	orange	qovoq rang
blue	kök	red	qizil
brown	jigar rang	white	oq
green	yashil	yellow	sariq

HEALTH

The quality of doctors and medical treatment is a little better than in many developing countries, but worse than in the western, industrialised countries. The majority of the doctors are trained in Uzbekistan, and most of them speak only one foreign language: Russian.

UZBEK

I'm sick.	men kasalman
My friend is sick.	mening döstim kasal
I need a doctor who speaks English.	men inglizcha sözlaidigan shifokorga muhtojman
I want a doctor that practises Chinese/western medicine.	men hitoi/gharb tibbiyotini qöllaidigan shifokorni istaiman
Can you bring a doctor to my room?	meninig honamga shifokorni olib kela olasizmi?
Please take me to a doctor.	iltimos meni shifokorga olib boring
I've been injured.	men jarohat kördim

I need an ambulance.	men tez yordamga muhtojman
Can you tell me where the ... is?	menga ... qaerdaligini aita olmaisizmi?
clinic	poliklinika
doctor	shifokor
hospital	kasalhona
nurse	hamshira
pharmacy	dorihona
I need an English interpreter.	men ingliz tarjimoniga muhtojman
I want a female doctor.	menga ayol shifokori zarur
Please use a new syringe.	iltimos yangi shprits ishlating
I have my own syringe.	mening özimning shpritsim bor
I'm not feeling well.	men özimni yakhshi his ëtmayapman
How long before it will get better?	qancha vaqtdan söng yakhshoroq böladi?

THE DOCTOR MAY SAY ...

nima böldi?	What's wrong?
qaeringiz oghriyapti?	Where does it hurt?
özingizni qandai his ëtyapsiz?	How are you feeling?
oghriq sezyapsizmi?	Do you feel any pain?
istimangiz bormi?	Do you have a temperature?
ötmishda qandai kasalliklarga duchor bölgansiz?	What illnesses have you had in the past?
chekasizmi?	Do you smoke?
ichasizmi?	Do you drink?
homiladormosiz?	Are you pregnant?
(bir) tabletkadan kuniga (tört) mahal iching	Take (1) tablet (4) times a day.
putur etgan erga kuniga (ikki) mahal suring	Apply to the affected area (twice) a day.
taomdan oldin/söng	before/after meal
uiqudan oldin	before bedtime

UZBEK

Parts of the Body

arm	qöl	kidney	buirak
bone	suyak	leg	son va oyoq
ear	quloq	liver	jigar
eye	köz	lung	öpka
face	yuz	mouth	oghiz
finger	barmoq	pulse	puls
foot	oyoq	skin	teri
hand	qöl	stomach	qorin
head	bosh	throat	tamogh
heart	yurak	urine	siydik

Ailments

I ...	men ...
have an insect bite	i hashorat chaqdi
can't move my ...	... bilan harakat qila olmaiman
can't sleep	uhlai olmaiman
have a heart condition	yurak hastaligi bor
have lost my appetite	ishtahamni yöqotdim
have missed my period for ... months.	mening kasalim ... oidan beri kelmayapti
am pregnant	homiladorman
vomited	qaid qilyapman/qusyapman
am weak	bemadorman
have a high pulse rate	-ing pulsim yuqori

I have ...	mening ... bor
altitude sickness	balandlik kasalligim
appendicitis	appenditsitim
asthma	astmam
diabetes	diabetim
diarrhoea	ichim ketyapti
dizziness	boshim ailanyapti
a fever	haroratim
hepatitis	sariq kasalim
an itch	qichishish
lice	bit

UZBEK

a migraine	bosh oghriq
a pain	oghriq
a stomachache	qorin oghrighi
venereal disease	teri kasalligim

I'm allergic to (antibiotics).   menda (antibiotiklarga) nisbatan allergiya bor

At the Chemist

May I have ... please?	iltimos menga ... bera olasizmi?
aspirin	aspirin
Band-Aids	bintlar
condoms	prezervativ
cough remedy	yötalga qarshi dori
eyedrops	köz uchun dori
insect repellent	hashoratlarni yaqinlashtirmaidigan dori
painkillers	oghriqni susaitiruvchi dori
sanitary napkins	sanitariya salfetkalari
sleeping pills	uiqu dorisi
contraceptive pills	homiladorlikga qarshi dori
travel sickness pills	sayohat kasalligiga qarshi dori

At the Dentist

dentist	tish shifokori
tooth/teeth	tish/tishlar
toothache	tash oghrighi
wisdom tooth	aql tishi
Is there a dentist here?	bu erda tish shifokori bormi?
I don't want it extracted.	buni sughurib tashlashingizni istamaiman
Please give me an anaesthetic.	iltimos menga anasteziya qiluvchi dori bering

Useful Words

accident	bahtsiz hodisa
acupuncture	akupunktura
AIDS	SPID
antibiotic	antibiotik
antiseptic	antiseptik

UZBEK

bandage	bint
blind	kör
blood (group/test)	qon (guruhi/tekshiruvi)
contraceptive	homiladorlikni oldini oluvchi dori
eye (drops)	köz (-uchun dori)
eye test	közni tekshirish
first aid	birinchi yordam
glasses	közoinaklar
injection	inëktsiya
menstruation	kasallik (menstruatsia)
optometrist	oftolmolog
pneumonia	pnevmoniya
Red Cross	qizil kirisit
specialist	mutahassis
surgeon	jarroh
syringe	shprits
virus	virus
vitamin	vitamin
X-ray	rentgen nurlari

TIME, DATES & FESTIVALS
Telling the time

When?	qachon?
What time is it?	soat necha böldi?
At what time?	soat hechada?

hour	soat
... o'clock	soat ...
half past ...	... yarim soat ötdi
minute	daqiqa
second	secund
a quarter	chorak
morning	ërtalab
in the afternoon	tushlikdan söng
noon	ön ikki
evening	oqshom
midnight	yarim kecha

UZBEK

Days of the Week

Sunday	yakshanba	Thursday	paishanba
Monday	dushanba	Friday	juma
Tuesday	seshanba	Saturday	shanba
Wednesday	chorshanba		

Months

January	yanvar	July	iyul
February	fevral	August	avgust
March	mart	September	sentyabr
April	aprel	October	oktyabr
May	mai	November	noyabr
June	iyun	December	dekabr

The Muslim Calendar

The Islamic calendar is lunar unlike the longer western solar calendar.

jaddi	saraton
dalv	asat
hut	sumbula
hamal	mezon
savr	aqrab
javzo	qavs

Present, Past & Future

today	bugun	last week	ötgan hafta
(this) week	(bu) hafta	last month	ötgan oi
tonight	bugungi oqshom	tomorrow	ërtaga
(this) month	(shu) oi	next week	kelasi hafta
yesterday	kecha	next month	keiingi oi
last night	kechagi kecha		

Festivals & Holidays

Independence Day – September 1. People gather in the main squares in each city. There are a lot of speeches by officials, parades, street performances, national music and dances, and flags flown.

Constitution Day – December 8

Women's day – March 8. On Women's Day, gifts are given to the female members of the family.

navruz – Oriental New Year, celebrated on March 21. On this day relatives, sons and daughters visit their parents, have meals, and spend the day together.

Day of Victory over fascist Germany – May 9

(Constitution Day and Victory Day are less significant).

ruza hait – the beginning of the month Ramadan in Arabic calendar. ruza hait is the beginning the Muslim fast. Families who lost a family member less than a year ago commemorate him or her by wearing national dresses (chopon, qyicha, and duppi) and sitting on the street. Friends and relatives get together to read the Koran.

kurban hait – the last day of the month Ramadan. This is celebrated in the same way as ruza hait. In addition, all the neighbours cook polo, and share with each other.

NUMBERS

0	nol	21	yigirma bir
1	bir	22	yigirma ikki
2	ikki	23	yigirma uch
3	uch	30	öttiz
4	tört	39	öttiz töqqiz
5	besh	40	qirq
6	olti	50	ëllik
7	etti	60	oltmish
8	sakkiz	70	etmish
9	töqqiz	80	sakson
10	ön	90	töqson
11	ön bir	100	bir yuz
12	ön ikki	101	bir yuz bir
13	ön uch	110	bir yuz ön
14	ön tört	115	bir yuz ön besh
15	ön besh	120	bir yuz yigirma
16	ön olti	190	bir yuz töqson
17	ön etti	200	ikki yuz
18	ön sakkiz	1000	ming
19	ön töqqiz	1001	ming bir
20	yigirma	10,000	ön ming

UZBEK

100,000	yuz ming
one million	bir million
10 million	ön million
100 million	yuz million
one billion	bir milliard

EMERGENCIES

Help!	yordamga!
Danger!	havf–hatar! (ëhtiyot böling!)
Don't move!	qimirlamang!
Stop.	töhtang
Go away.	keting
Listen, we're not interested.	quloq soling, bizni bu qiziqtirmaidi
Call the police.	militsiyaga qönghiroq qiling
Call a doctor.	shofokorga qönghiroq qiling
Could you help me please?	iltimos menga yordam bering
There has been an accident.	bahtsiz hodisa yuz berdi
I've been injured.	men jarohat kördim
I've been raped.	men zörlashdi
I've been robbed.	meni tunashdi
Could I please use the telephone?	iltimos telefondan foidalansom böladimi?
I wish to contact my embassy.	özimning ëlchihomaga qönghiroq qilishni istaiman

UZBEK

Kyrgyz

KYRGYZ

INTRODUCTION

Kyrgyz is spoken by 2.75 million in Central Asia, Russia and China. The majority of these speakers (around 2.3 million) are inhabitants of Kyrgyzstan. The language is spoken in areas lying to the east and northeast of the regions where Uzbek is spoken. It's a language that has been preserved by the high mountains and deep valleys that are home to Kyrgyz speakers and to those groups who retreated to this region for the security it provides. The Kyrgyz diaspora is found in Uzbekistan (180,000), Xinjiang, China (150,000), Tajikistan (70,000), Russia (45,000) and Kazakhstan (15,000).

PRONUNCIATION

Kyrgyz is written in the Cyrillic script in Kyrgyzstan and a modified Persian-Arabic script in China. Both the Soviet and Chinese governments imposed changes from Arabic to Cyrillic and Roman scripts in the hope of breaking the Kyrgyz ties to the Muslim world.

Most Kyrgyz sounds are found in the English language while a few additional ones must be learned. Intonation is important and can be learned by listening to Kyrgyz speak. The Kyrgyz and Kazakh languages are slurred, spoken quickly, and are so close that those who use Kyrgyz to speak to a Kazakh will likely be asked why they are speaking Kazakh with a Kyrgyz accent.

Vowels

There are 10 vowels in the Kyrgyz language and almost all correspond to English sounds except the sounds ö and ü which are produced with rounded lips. Like the Turkish language, both the Kyrgyz and Kazakh languages are characterised by vowel harmony in which a word's vowels match as in tüshündüm ('I understand') and ulunguz ('your ethnic group').

Double vowels such as uu, aa, and oo indicate a lengthening in pronunciation.

Kyrgyz Language Area

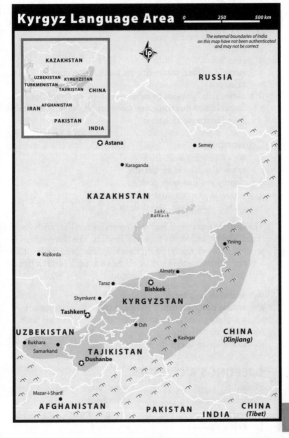

a   as in 'father'
ä   as in 'sat'
e   as in 'bet'
ë   as the 'ye' sound in 'yet'
i   as in 'bill'
o   as in 'go'
ö   as the 'e' in 'her' made with the well rounded lips
u   as in 'put'
ü   as the 'i' in 'bit' with rounded and pushed forward lips
y   found in between consonants, sounds like 'e' in 'sister' and is
     found in the word 'Kyrgyz'

Consonants

h   with aspiration as in 'haste'
j   as the 's' in 'vision' or 'treasure'
p   slightly muffled as in 'push'
q   a hard 'k' as in the Arab country 'Qatar'
r   slightly trilled, soft, and close to an 'l' sound

The consonants written with two letters (cluster) are fairly easy to
learn. The ch and sh are found in English. The three other clusters will take practice but if they are too difficult in the beginning
you can pronounce the gh as an 'r', the kh as an 'h', and zh like a 'j'
and you will eventually be understood.

ch   as the 'ch' in 'cheek'
gh   similar to the French 'r' (see page 16 for an explanation)
kh   a slightly guttural sound like the 'ch' in the Scottish 'loch'
ng   as the 'ng' in 'rung'
sh   as the 'sh' in 'sheep'

GREETINGS & CIVILITIES

Please.	chaqëruu
Please sit down.	olturunguz
Thank you.	chong rakhmat
Excuse/Pardon me.	kechiresiz

KYRGYZ

Men shake hands, but the only women who do so are business women. To show respect some men use two hands to shake and use the left hand to pat the top of the other's right hand. A recent handshake innovation is to use the left hand to pat the other's shoulder. Men in southern Kyrgyzstan place their right hand on their hearts for a greeting.

When women see their friends from afar they begin to bow slightly and as they near greetings are shared while bowing slightly and energetically from the head and shoulders. Women sometimes greet by touching right cheek to right cheek without kissing the cheek. Older women will place a puckered kiss on the cheek of younger women. It's polite for younger and foreign women to kiss elderly women on the cheeks.

Never mind.	kerek jok
Correct.	tuura/durus
Good.	jaqshë
OK.	maqul
That will do.	bolot
Do you understand?	tüshündüngüzbü?
No.	joq
Yes.	oshondoy/ooba
I understand.	tüshündüm
I don't understand.	tüshünbödüm
Sorry.	kechiresiz
No problem.	ech nerse emes
Please wait awhile.	kichine kütöturunguz
Where's the toilet?	daaratqanasë qayerde?

Greetings & Goodbyes

Good morning/day/evening.	assalamu aleykum
	(lit: peace be upon you)
And upon you peace.	wa aleykum assalam
Good night.	tününgüz beypil bolsun

KYRGYZ

How are you?	abalëngëz qanday?/ishter qanday?
How is your health?	den soolyghungëz qanday?
Fine, (and you?)	jaqshë, (özüungüz qandaysëz?)
Not bad.	jaman emes
Have you eaten?	tamaq tandëngëzbë?
Where are you going?	kayda barasëz?
What are you doing?	emne qëlëp jatasëz?
Goodbye.	qosh
See you tomorrow.	(erteng) körüshkönchö
Have a good trip.	aq jol bolsun
See you soon.	körüshörbüz
You've been a great help.	siz abdan chong jardam berdingiz

• The Kyrgyz employ many sounds to express meaning. As they are listening to someone, they may make the sounds un hun, aah (a rising sound) or mmm. To say no, they use uh uh with a shaking of the head from side to side. To express surprise, 'really?', or 'wow', some say ahyee but in villages oy voy yuy is more commonly heard. The sound oy is like 'oops' when you make a mistake. To express pain, Kyrgyz make the grunting sound hunh, and say oof when very tired. When they are disappointed the sound ääh is emitted, and the sound öf is used to express something that is terrible or disgusting.

• To apologise Kyrgyz touch their chests with their right or both hands flat to the chest. This right hand touch to the heart is also used when serving tea or expressing welcome. To beckon someone, the hand is held palm up with fingers curling back repeatedly. Another gesture is made shaming someone for doing bad, which is to pinch one's own cheek or rub one's own cheek downward to express that the person has no face or shame, 'beting jok'.

• In order to attract attention, Kyrgyz raise their hands and say kechiresiz, and in more urgent situations they yell ay!

KYRGYZ

Language Difficulties

Do you speak English?	englische süylöyalasëzbë?
I don't speak English.	men anglische süylöyalbaymën
I don't speak Kyrgyz.	kyrgzche süylöyalbaymën
Do you have an interpreter?	qotormochungar barbë?
How do you say that in Kyrgyz?	munu kyrgyzche emne deyt?
Can you repeat that please?	kaytalasangëz?
Could you speak louder/	qatuuraq/jayëraq
slower please?	ündösüylöngüz?
Please point to the word/	bul kitepten bul sözdü/
phrase in the book.	süylömdükörsötüp bersengiz
Just a minute.	azër
What does it mean?	anën maanisi emne?

SMALL TALK
Meeting People

What's your name?	atëngëz kim?
What's your father's name?	atangëzdën atë emne?
Who are you?	siz kim bolosuz?
I'm pleased to meet you.	siz menen taanëshqanëma
	qubanëchtuumun
So am I.	men da ötöqubanëchtuumun
What time is it?	azër saat qancha boldu?
What is this?	bul emne?
Are your parents living?	ata-enengiz barbë?
My (mother) is alive but my	(apam) bar, biroq (atam) joq
(father) is not.	

Nationalities

What country are you from?	qaysë mamleketten keldingiz?
What ethnic group do you	ulutunguz emne?
come from?	
I come from (the USA).	(amerikadan) keldim

KYRGYZ

Age

How old are you?	qancha jashtasëz?
How old do you think I am?	qancha jashta dep oyloysuz?
I think you are (35) years old.	ottuz (beshte dirsiz)

Religion

As there are many ethnic groups in Kyrgyzstan, Kyrgyz group strangers along the lines of the ethnic groups they resemble. Those looking like Russians will be associated with Christianity, those resembling Arabs or Pakistanis will be considered Muslims. But Kyrgyz don't often ask those they don't know about their religious beliefs.

I am (a) ...	men ... -ge/gha/ne ishenemin
Buddhist	buddizim
Catholic	katolik dini
Christian	hristian dini
Hindu	india dini
Jewish	eudaizim
Muslim	islam dini

I'm not religious.	men dinge ishenbeym
Do you attend Mosque?	siz mechitke barasëzbë?

Family

This is my ...	bul menin ...
father/mother	atam/apam (enem)
husband/wife	küyööm/ayalëm
	(qoluqtuum)
girlfriend/boyfriend	süygönüm
son/daughter	uulum/qëzëm
younger brother/sister	inim/singdim
older brother/sister	agham ejem

Are you married? (m)	üylöngönsüzbü?
Are you married? (f)	turmushqa chëqkansëzbë?
I'm married.	üylöngöm
I'm single.	men boydoqmun
How many children do you have?	qancha balangiz bar?

I don't have any children.	balam joq
How many brothers/sisters do you have?	sizdin qancha agha-iningiz bar?
I don't have any brothers/sisters.	agha-ini/eje-singdim joq

GETTING AROUND

I'd like to go to ...	men ... barmaqmën
How can I get to ...?	men emne menen ... baralam?
Which bus do I take to get to ...?	men qaysë aptobuz menen ... baralam?
Is there another way to get there?	bashka jol barbë?

What time does the next ... leave/arrive?	keler kiyinkisi ... qachan kelet/chighat?
bus	aptobuz
train	poyuz
plane	samolyot

Where is the ...?	... qayerde?
airport	ayeroport
bus stop	aptobuz ayaldamasë
bus terminal	uzun jolduu aptobus ayaldamasë
train station	poyuz istansiasë
ticket office	belet satuu ordu

Is it far?	alësbë?
Yes, it's far.	ooba, alës
It's quite close.	abdan jaqën
Can I walk there?	bul jerden te tigil jergechein barsa bolobu?
How much time will it take to walk there?	jööjürsö qancha ubaqët ketet?
What's the address?	adresingiz?
Please write down the address for me.	magha anën adresin jazip beringiz

| Could you tell the taxi driver the address please? | taksi shoopuruna bul adresti aytëp bersengiz? |
| Please draw a map for me. | magha kartasën sëzëp beringiz |

Directions

To indicate distance, Kyrgyz raise their voice pitch – the higher the pitch the farther the distance. To show a direction, Kyrgyz either point with their index fingers or with an open palm.

Which direction?	qaysë baghëtta?
Go straight ahead.	tüz keteberingiz
Turn right/left.	onggho/solgo buruluu

direction	baghët
east/west	chëghësh/batësh
north/south	tündük/tüshtük
southeast	tüshtük chëghësh
northwest	tündük batësh
uphill/downhill	too üstü/booru
left/right	sol/ong
at the corner	burulushta
up/down	üstü/tömön(kübölük)
upstairs/downstairs	üstünküqabat/astënqëqabat
far away	alës (alësta)
outside/inside	sërtënda/ichinde (ichi)
middle	orto/ortodo
near/near to ...	jaqën/jaqënda ...
that/this direction	al/bul jaq

Buying Tickets

Where is the ticket office?	belet satuu ordu qayerde?
I would like a (first class) ticket to (Osh).	magha (osh) gha bara turghan (birinchi darajaluu) bilet kerek
How much is the train to (Talas)?	(talas)ge chein bilet qancha turat?

Is there a ticket for the bus to Narën today?	bügün (narën)ga baruu üchün bilet barbë?
What's the cheapest fare to (Bishkek)?	(bishkek)ge baruu üchün eng arzan bilet qaysë?
There are no tickets.	bilet joq

berth number	orun nomuru
berth upper/lower	joghorqu (tömönkü) orun
cancelled	toqtotulghan
confirm	bolot dep bilüü
dormitory bunk	karawat
economy class	ëqtësade bölüm
second class	ekinchi iretki
first class	birinchi daraja
no room	üy joq
one-way ticket	taq jolduu belet
return tickets	baruu-kelüübeleti
refund	pul tölöö
seat	orun
student's ticket	oquuchular beleti
ticket office	belet satuu ordu
timetable	ubaqët jadëbalë

Air

I want to confirm my flight.	beletimdi okey qëldëram
This price is higher than normal.	bul baa adettekiden joghoru

aeroplane	samolyot
airline ticket	samolyottun bileti
customs' (declaration)	tamojna (malëmatë)
departure	ayrëluu
estimated time of arrival/ departure	jolgho chëghuu/jetip baruu ubaq të
gate number	eshik nomuru
no smoking	tameki check beng
passport	pasport

Bus

Kyrgyz buses, especially in Bishkek, are crowded and noisy during rush hour. Pickpockets, particularly those that use knives to slice open purses and bags, are to be watched for.

Is this going to the (bazaar)?	bul (bazargha) barabë?
I want to get off at ...	menda ... baram.
Please tell me when we've reached that stop.	al beketke qachan jetip barar?

bus (stop/terminal)	aptobuz (ayaldamasë/stansiasë)
long-distance bus station	usun jolduu aptobuz stansiasë

Train

Can you help me find my seat/berth please?	ordumdu tabëshëp berish sengiz?
Excuse me, this is my seat.	kechiresiz, bul menin ordum
Where is the dining car?	ashqana wagon qayerde?

dining car	poyuzdun ashqana wagonu
express train	ayrëqcha ëldam poyuz
fast train	ëldam poyuz
hard seat (2nd class)	qatuu orunduq
hard-sleeper (2nd class)	qatuu karawat
soft-seat (1st class)	jumshaq karawat
train	poyuz

Taxi

To flag down a taxi, you hold your arm straight out to the side with the relaxed hand palm down. There are no meters in the taxis because of the difficulty in standardising fares due to inflation, so all fares must be negotiated beforehand. Drivers are not tipped. Men sit in front of the cab, women and children in the back. Some freelance drivers are available to take fares but visitors are advised that such drivers may be involved in robbery schemes. It's best not to pick up others who may flag your taxi or car down in the street.

I'd like to go to ...	men ... ge barat elem
How long does it take to go to ...?	... ge baruugha qanchalëq ubaqët ketet?

Are any English-speaking drivers available?	anglische bile turghan shoopur barbë?
How much?	qancha turat?
Thank you.	ëraqmat
Please stop here.	bul jerde toqtonguz
First go to the station, then the airport.	aldëmenen beketke, anan ayeroportgo baram
Stop at the next corner.	daghëbir burulushta toqtonguz
Please hurry.	ëldamëraak bolunguz
Please slow down.	astalangë
Please wait here.	bul jerde toktup turungus
I'll get off here.	men ushul jerden tüshöm
Where can I hire a taxi?	qayerden taksi ijara alalam?
How much is it for one/three day(s)?	bir/üch kündügü qancha pul?

Useful Words

accident	qërsëq
air conditioning	aba tengshegich
battery	bataria
bicycle	welosiped
brake	tormuz
car	mashina
driver's licence	shoopurluq kenishkesi
engine oil	mashine mayë
fill up	tolturup may quyuu
flat tyre	rezinke dönggölök
headlight	aldëngqëchëraq
highway	joghoru süröttüütash jol
international driving licence	el aralëq shopurluq kenishkesi
map	qarëyta
motorbike	motosikil
parking	toqtotuu
petrol	benizin
radiator	radiator
service station	teylööordu
taxi rental	taksi ijaragha aluu

KYRGYZ

towing a car	mashineni suroo
traffic jam	qatnash tosulup qaluu
traffic signs	qatnash belgisi
tyre	dönggölök

ACCOMMODATION

hotel/inn	mëymanqana
apartment	bölmö
dormitory	jataqana
guesthouse	qonoq üy
youth hostel	jashtar mëymanqanasë
campsite	söör/supoo/bastërma

It's possible to stay with local Kyrgyz families. The fee must be negotiated and it depends on the economic status of the family. A wealthy family may refuse to receive payment altogether but in such cases you shouldn't expect any kind of services. A family of more modest means might cook meals, do laundry and go shopping for you. Foreign guests should give gifts that represent part of their own culture.

Where is a guesthouse?	mëymanqana qayerde
I'd like to book a room.	men aldënala numurgha (bölmöghö) zakaz qëlayën dedim ele

I'm looking for a ... hotel.	men ... mëymanqanasën izdep jüröm
cheap	arzan
clean	pakiz
good	jaqshë
near-the-city	shaardën janënda
near-the-airport	ayrodromdun janënda
nearby	jaqën jerde

Booking a Room

As yet the hotels in Kyrgyzstan are not up to high international standards. Hotels often have different levels of lodgings on various floors.

Some floors may have antique furnishings, others cheap and poorly maintained. It's important to find out what rooms are furnished with, as showers, refrigerators or televisions may not be standard.

Do you have any rooms available?	bosh bölmö barbë?
Do you have any beds available?	qarawat barbë?

I would like a ...	magha ... kerek
single/twin room	jalghëz/eki kishilik bölmö
quiet room	tënch bölmö
big room	chong bölmö
(double) bed	(eki jayluu) karawat

At the Hotel

How much is it per night?	bir tünösö qancha bolot?
How much is it per person?	bir kishiligi qancha bolot?
Is there a discount for students/children?	oquuchugha/baldargha etibar berilebi?
Can I get a discount if I stay longer?	uzunuraq tursam baada etibar berilebi?
Are there any cheaper ones?	arzanëraaghënan barbë?
Can I see the room first?	aldëmenen üydükörsöm boloby?
Are there any others?	bashqasë barbë?
I like this/that room.	bolot eken/ushul üydüalayën
It's fine, I'll take this room.	men turayën dep jatam

I am going to stay for ...	men ... tünöyüm
one/two night(s)	bir/eki kün
a few days	bir neche kün
a week	bir juma

Can I have the key please?	achqëchtë magha beresizbi?
Is hot water available all day?	jëluu suu ar dayëm barbë?
Could I have a different room?	bashqa üy alsam bolobu?
Any messages for me?	magha qabarlarë barbë?
Please do not disturb.	ubaqtëmdë albangëz

KYRGYZ

Requests & Complaints

It's too ...	bul ötöele ...
big/small	chong/kichinekey
hot/cold	ëssëq/suuq
dark/dirty	qarangghë/kir
noisy	ëzë-chuu

It smells.	bir nerse jëttanat
The toilet/sink is blocked.	daaratqana/qol jughuch tëqëlëp qalëptër
The door is locked.	eshik jabëlëp qalëptër
My room number is (123).	bölmö nomurum (bir jüz jëyërma üch)
Please fix it as soon as possible.	munu ëldamëraaq ornotup bering

Checking Out

I'd like to check out now/ tomorrow.	men eseptesh mekmin azër/ erteng
I'd like to pay the bill.	men talongho pul tölöymün
Can I leave my luggage here for a few days?	jügümdüushul jerde birneche kün qoysom boloby?
Thank you for your hospitality.	mëyman dostughunguz üchün raqmat

I'm returning ...	men ... qaytamën
tomorrow	erteng
in 2-3 days	eki-üch kündö
next week	narqë(keler) jumada

Useful Words

address	adres	key	achqë(achqëch)
baggage	somke	light bulb	lampochka
balcony	balkon	lobby	karidor
basin	das	lock	qulpu
bathroom	moncho	reception desk	teylöösekisi
bed	karawat	room	bölmö
bill	talon	shower	dush
blanket	juurkan, töshök	sleeping bag	uqtoo qaltasë
bucket	chelek	toilet	daaratqana

KYRGYZ

AROUND TOWN

Bishkek is a town blessed with trees. It's also very cosmopolitan with 82 different ethnic groups. While there are several main streets in the business part of town, most buildings are only four to five stories because of earthquakes which occur, on average, twice a month.

In Bishkek and the rural areas, most men wear western dress. The topuskullcap has gained popularity since independence. Women wear headscarves which is also a recent introduction.

At the Bank

account	esep
amount	esep summasë
buying rate	satëp aluu narqë
cash	naq pul
cashier	kassir
cheque	pul chegi
credit card	ötümdüü kartochka
deposit	amanat kötegi
exchange (rate)	almashtëruu (baasë)
foreign currency	chetel aqchasë
money exchange	aqcha almashtruu
official rate	ökümöt baasënda
receipt	öjöt
signature	imza/qol
travellers' cheque	sayakhat chegi
withdrawal	qaytarëp saluu

At the Post Office

Post office service in Kyrgyzstan is notorious as only half the mail gets through. Most of the workers are non-Kyrgyz which is somewhat understandable because the population of Bishkek is half non-Kyrgyz. Both Russian and English are spoken in Bishkek's post offices. Although extremely expensive, Bishkek is now serviced by some international couriers.

KYRGYZ

I'd like to send ... to (Australia).	men ... (awstralia)gha jibermekchimin
How much is it?	baasë qancha?
How much does this weigh?	salmaghë qancha?

address	adress	post code	pochta nomuru
aerogram	ayrogram	post office	pochtoqana
airmail	aviapochta	poste restante	do vostrebov-
envelope	konwert		aniya
fax	faks	registered mail	zakaz qat
insurance	qamsëzdandëruu	stamps	marka
letter	qat	surface mail	adetteki qat
parcel	pasëlka	(urgent)	(chuqul)
postcard	atkirtka	telegram	telegramma

Telephone

I want to make a phone call. to (Canada)	(kanada)gha telefon chalam
What's the number?	telefon nomuru qancha?
The number is ...	telefon nomuru ...
Hello (phone use).	allo
Can I speak to ...?	... menen süylösh söm bolobu?

collect call	abonent tölööchüü telefon chaluu
country code	ölkökodu
directory	telefon nomer depteri
engaged	telefon bosh emes
international call	el aralëq telefon
public telephone	telefon-avtomat
telephone (number)	telefon (nomuru)
wrong number (recorded phone message)	qata nomur (nomur tuura emes alëndë)

Sightseeing

Kyrgyzstan is filled with places to visit but less well-known is that nightlife in Bishkek is also exciting. Besides the disco bars, there are casinos and cabaret shows. Restaurants serve good, inexpensive food. Cinemas mainly show films from the USA and India, but

KYRGYZ

sometimes show Kyrgyzstan films which were quite excellent up to the break up of the Soviet Union. Theatre in Bishkek is very good, showing international hits and performed by very talented actors. If you want to ask what there is to do in the evening just ask: gechinde emne qëlalë?

What's the name of this place?	bul jerdi emne dep atayt?
Excuse me, what is this/that?	kechiresiz, bul/al emne?
Do you have a local map?	sizde jergiliktüü karta barbë?
Am I allowed to take photos here?	bul jerde süröt tartsam bolobu?
What time does it open/close?	qachan achëlat/jabëlat?

How much is the ...?	... qancha turat?
admission fee	belet baasë
guidebook	sayaqat qoldonmosu
postcard	atkrëtka

ancient	ilgerki	ruins	qaldëqtarë
archaeology	arkheologia	sculpture	skulptura
building	imarat	sightseeing	ekiskursa qëluu
monument	estelik munarasë	souvenirs	estelik buyum
museum	muzey	statue	aykel
old city	eski shaar	theatres	teatërqana

IN THE COUNTRY

Travelling alone in the countryside is considered dangerous as there are no established places to stay, although travelling with Kyrgyz is relatively safe. No agencies are responsible for travel to outlying villages beyond the more well-trodden routes. However, if you want to walk around in a small village you should ask somebody; men sizdin aylingizdi gorup chiksam bolobu? 'Is it alright for me to look around your village?.'

Weather

What's the weather like today/ tomorrow?	bügün/erte aba ërayë qanday?
The weather's nice today.	bügün aba ërayë jaqshë
Will it rain tomorrow?	erteng jamghër jaaybë?

KYRGYZ

It's hot.	ëssëq
It's raining.	jamghër jaap jatat

It's ...	aba ...
fine/wet	jaqshë/nëm
clear/cloudy	buluttuu
dark/sunny	bürköö/nurluu (achëq)
very cold/hot	ötösuuq/ötöëssëq
very windy	boroon

flood	sel	snow	qar	
fog	tuman	sunrise	kün chëghuu	
lightning	chaghëlghan	sunset	kündün batëshë	
mud	batqaq	thunder	chaghëlghan	
rain	jamghër	weather	abaa ërayë	
sky	asman	wind	shamal	

Along the Way

When do we go?	qachan jolgho chëghabëz?
Where are we?	biz qayerdebiz?
Can you please tell me how to get to ...?	...jerge kantip jetsem bolot?
What will we pass on the way?	joldo qayerlerden ötöbüz?
How far is it from here to ...?	bul jerden ...ge qanchalëq aralëq bar?
Are there any things to see?	bul jerde körüügötiyeshelüüemne bar?
Let's take a rest here.	bul jerde dem alalë
Can I have a cup of water/tea?	bir stakan suu/chay barbë?

Seasons

spring	jaz	autumn	küz	
summer	jay	winter	qësh	
cave	üngkür	earth	batqaq/jersharë	
country	ayel	earthquake	jertitiröö	
desert	qumduq chöl	farm	ayël charsë	

farmer	deyqan	mudslide	qëyan
high plateau	döng	public toilet	daarataqana
hill	adër	river	darëya
hot springs	arashan/ëssëk bulak	road	jol
		rock	too tek
lake	köl	seasons	jël mezgilderi
landslide	too jemirilüü	valley	jëlgha
map	karta	village	qështaq
mountain (range/trail)	too (rayon/ jolu)	well	quduq

Animals & Birds

In the countryside the most common animals seen are cows, horses, chickens, sheep, geese, ducks, cats and dogs. Beware of vicious dogs and of horses that may kick and bite.

camel	töö	mare	bee
cat	mëshëk	monkey	maymë
dog	it	parrot	papugay
donkey	eshek	pigeon	baqtek
duck	örgök	rat	ar-chëchqan
goat	echki	sheep	qoy
hen	tooq	swallow	chabalekey
horse	jëlqë	yak	topoz
goose	kaz		

FOOD

Villagers sit on the floor to eat at short-legged tables with men, sitting cross legged and women with their legs tucked behind them on one side. The main dish is placed in the centre of the table. In the city, Kyrgyz eat at regular dining tables as in European countries. At a large gathering, the most respected or eldest male at the meal will sit at the head of the table. Moving away from him, men sit in descending order of rank with women at the far side of the table. In southern Kyrgyzstan, men will eat together in one room with women and children in another. Kyrgyz in rural areas sometimes eat with their hands or with spoons. In regions closer to Xinjiang chopsticks are frequently used. For funerals or for weddings, a large horse will be slaughtered and eaten.

KYRGYZ

food stall	azëk-tülük
market	bazar
bar	bar/araqqana
Chinese/Korean restaurant	qëtay/korealëq restoran
Chinese Muslim restaurant	dungan restoran
tea house	chayqana
restaurant	restoran

I want to go to a restaurant with Kyrgyz/Chinese food.	men kyrgyzcha/qëtaycha restorangha baramën

At the Restaurant

Can I see the menu, please?	tamaq tizmesin körsöm bolobu?
I'll try that.	men ushul (tamqdë) qaalaym
I'd like what he's eating.	men aldëmdagh ëgishinikindey tamaq qaalayt elem
Do you have an English menu?	anglische tamaqtin tizmesi barbë?
Can you recommend any dishes?	qanday jaqshë tamaq tarëngëz bar?
Do you have a knife and fork?	bëchaq jana beshilingiz barbë?
The bill please.	eseptesheli
I don't eat meat.	et jebeymin

I'd like to have ...	... jeymin/ichemin
pilaf	palou
food	tamaq
noodles	kesme/makaron
beverages	suusunduq
alcoholic drinks	araq
rice	gürüch
bread	nan

beshbarmak	meat with noodles
dimlama	steamed layers of meat and vegetables topped with cabbage

langmen	boiled noodles		
mantë	steamed buns stuffed with meat and onions		
pilmeni	wonton soup		

Breakfast, Lunch & Dinner

| breakfast | ertengmenki tamaq | dinner | kechki tamaq |
| lunch | tüshkütamaq | snack | qoshumcha tamaq |

bread	nan	tea	chay
eggs	jumurtqa	yoghurt	ayran
milk	süt		

Kyrgyz drink tea with milk and salt or, sometimes, with jam. In Bishkek, Kyrgyz eat a more European type of breakfast with coffee, juice, bread and cheese, sometimes a fried egg or fruit.

Lunch is lighter than the evening dinner meal. It normally consists of bread, sausage and cheese. Milk products such as cottage cheese, buttered bread, milk and yoghurt are eaten.

Dinner is the central meat meal served with vegetables. Pilaf rice is sometimes served but more often noodles. Nan, a flat bread, is cooked in a tandër, a beehive-shaped oven.

SHOPPING

Bazaars are where the best shopping is had. Here you can find the freshest vegetables at the best prices. Kyrgyz merchants tend not to be pushy but they will bargain the price. When finalising a deal, they'll ask, makulbu? ('OK?'). If you agree, reply makul

How many/much?	qancha turat/pul?
I'd like to buy ...	men ... almaqchëmën
I'm just looking.	man jönele qarap jatam
How much does this/that cost?	bul/al qancha turat?
That's very expensive/cheap.	al qëmbat/arzan eken
Can you reduce the price?	arzanëraaq beresiz bi?
Where can I buy a ...?	... di qayerden alalam?

Where's the nearest ...?	eng jaqën jerdegi ... qayerde?
bazaar	bazar
store	magezin
market	bazar

KYRGYZ

Sizes & Quantities

a bottle of	bötölkö	one metre/litre	bir metr/litr
half a dozen	jarëmetr	two kilometres	eki kilometr

Colours

black	qara	orange	qëzël-sarë
blue	kök	red	qëzël
brown	küröng	white	aq
green	jashël	yellow	sarë

HEALTH

Kyrgyz doctors are reputed to be excellent. Most have been trained at the Kyrgyz State Medical Institute and speak Russian and Kyrgyz. Because of the lack of medical diagnostic technology, those faced with complicated and serious illnesses should leave the country for care. Major western embassies have their own clinics.

I'm sick.	oorup qaldëm
My friend is sick.	dosum oorup qaldë
I need a doctor.	doqturgha körünömün
I need a doctor who can speak English.	maghan anglische bileturghan doqtur kerek
I want a Kyrgyz doctor.	men kyrgyz doqtur kerek
I want a doctor that practises western/Chinese medicine.	maghan ewropacha/qëtaycha darëlayturghan doqtur kerek
Can you bring a doctor to my room?	jataqanama doqtur chaqërëp kelsengiz?
Please take me to a doctor.	meni doqturgha alëp barsangëz
I've been injured.	men jaraqat aldëm
I need an ambulance.	magha tez jardam mashënasë kerek
Can you tell me where the ... is?	magha ... qayerde ekemin aytëp beralasëzbë?
clinic	darëloo bölümü
doctor	doqtur

KYRGYZ

hospital	doqturqana
nurse	medsestra
pharmacy	darëqana

I need an English interpreter.	maghan anglische qotormochu kerek
I want a female doctor.	maghan ayal doqtur kerek
Please use a new syringe.	janghë shpiris ishtetsengiz
I have my own syringe.	mende shpiris bar
I don't want a blood transfusion.	men qan quydurbaymën
I'm not feeling well.	men özümdü jaman sezip turam
How long before it will get better?	saqayuugha qancha ubaqët këtët?

THE DOCTOR MAY SAY ...

emne boldu?	What's wrong?
qayeringiz oorup jatat?	Where does it hurt?
qandaysëz?	How are you feeling?
oorup jatabë?	Do you feel any pain?
denengiz ësëp turabë?	Do you have a temperature?
murda emne oorunghuz bar ele?	What illnesses have you had in the past?
tameki chegesizbi?	Do you smoke?
araq ichesizbi?	Do you drink?
boyunguzda barbë?	Are you pregnant?

Parts of the Body

arm	qol	foot	but
bone	söök	hand	qol
ear	qulaq	head	bash
eye	köz	heart	jürök
face	bet	kidney	böyrök
finger	manjalar	leg	but

KYRGYZ

liver	boor	skin	teri
lung	öpkö	stomach	qarën/ashqazan
mouth	ooz	throat	tamaq
pulse	qan tamër	urine	siydik

Ailments

I ...	men ...
have an insect bite	qurt-qumursqa chaghëp aldë
can't sleep	uyqu joq
have a heart condition	jürögüm ooruu
have lost my appetite	tamaq jegim kelbeyt
have missed my period for ... months.	... aydan beri etek kirimdi köröelekmin
have a high pulse rate	tamërëm tez soghup jatat
am pregnant	boyumda bar
vomited	qustum
am weak	ajëz

I have ...	men ...
altitude sickness	tooluu jerden bolochu ooruu
asthma	astma
diabetes	diabet
diarrhoea	ich ötkök
dizziness	bash aylanuu
a fever	temperatura
hepatitis	boor oorusu
an itch	jel
lice	bit
a migraine	qatuu bash ooruu
a pain	ooruu
a stomachache	ich oorusu
venereal disease	jënës oorusu

I'm allergic to (antibiotics).   menim (antibiotikter)ge alergiyam bar

At the Chemist

May I have ... please?	magha ... barbeken
aspirin	aspirin
condoms	prezervativ
cough remedy	jötöldün darësë
eyedrops	köz darësë
insect repellent	chaqchuu jolotpo üchün sëypalghan darëmay
painkiller	ooru toqtutuu darësë
sanitary napkins	gigiyencheskie prokladki
sleeping pills	uykunun darësë
contraceptive pills	boygho bütüüdön saqtoochu darë
travel sickness pills	jürök aylanganda icheturghan darë

At the Dentist

dentist	tish doqturu
tooth/teeth	tish/tishter
toothache	tish oorusu
wisdom tooth	aqël tish
Is there a dentist here?	bul jerde tish doqturu barbë?
I don't want it extracted.	tishimdi suurutbaymën
Please give me an anaesthetic.	magha narkoz beringiz

Useful Words

accident	iyne sayuu
acupuncture	akupunktura
AIDS	SPID
antibiotic/antiseptic	antibiotik/antiseptik
blind	kör/soqur
blood (test/group)	qan (teksherüü/tibi)
contraceptive	töröttün aldën alaturghan
doctor	doqtur
eye (drops/test)	köz (darësë/teksherüü)
first aid	tez qutqazun

glasses	köz aynek	specialist	kesptik doqtur
injection	ökül saluu	surgeon	hirurq
menstruation	etek kir kelüü	syringe	ishpirits
optometrist	közildirik saluuchu	virus	virus
		vitamin	vitamin
pneumonia	öpköseskenüüsü	X-ray	rentgin nuru
Red Cross	qëzël kirist		

TIME, DATES & FESTIVALS

Telling the Time

When? qachan?
What time is it? azër saat qancha boldu?

hour	saat	afternoon	tüshtön kiyin
... o'clock	saat ...	noon	tüsh
half past ...	jarëm saat ...	evening	kech
a quarter	bir cheerek	midnight	tün ortosu
morning	erteng menen		

Days of the Week

Sunday	jekshenbi	Thursday	beyshenbi
Monday	düyshümbü	Friday	juma
Tuesday	sheyshenbi	Saturday	ishenbi
Wednesday	charshenbi		

Months

January	yanwar	July	iyul
February	fewral	August	awghust
March	mart	September	sentabër
April	aprel	October	öktöbür
May	may	November	noyabër
June	iyun	December	dekabër

Present, Past & Future

| today | bügün | (this) week | (bul) juma |
| tonight | kechinde | (this) month | (bul) ay |

KYRGYZ

yesterday	kechee	tomorrow	erteng
last week	ötkön juma	next week	keler juma
last night	keche kechinde	next month	keler ay
last month	ötkön ay		

Festivals & Holidays

January 1 – New Year's Day

January 7 – Russian Orthodox Christmas

March 8 – International Women's Day – celebrated by presenting women with gifts.

March 21 – naw roz – Spring Solstice celebrated throughout the Persian-speaking world and recently introduced in Kyrgyzstan after the Soviet breakup. Bishkek plays host to parades in the main square, that is decked out in flowers and balloons.

May 9 – Victory Day – Celebration of victory over the Fascists in Europe during WWII, with military parades.

August 31 – Independence Day – Commemorates the independence of Kyrgyzstan from the Soviet Union.

September 1 – Day of Knowledge (ilm gunu) – The first day of school for students of all ages in which they register and bring flowers to their teachers.

orozo ayt – Marks the ends of Ramadan, the month-long Islamic fast. During this day, Kyrgyz commemorate their dead relatives.

korban ayt – Islamic festival commemorating Ibrahim's attempted sacrifice of his son on Mount Moriah where God supplied a sheep instead. Kyrgyz usually sacrifice a black sheep during this holiday which is done for the sake of the living. Families invite Islamic scholars to read passages from the Koran to family members. Elders bring money to the mosque and ask that religious scholars say prayers for their living family members.

Numbers

0	nöl	5	besh	10	on	15	on besh
1	bir	6	altë	11	on bir	16	on altë
2	eki	7	jeti	12	on eki	17	on jeti
3	üch	8	segiz	13	on üch	18	on segiz
4	tört	9	toghuz	14	on tört	19	on toghuz

KYRGYZ

20	jëyërma	110	bir jüz on
21	jëyërma bir	115	bir jüz on besh
22	jëyërma eki	120	bir jüz jëyërma
23	jëyërma üch	190	bir jüz toqson
30	otuz	200	eki jüz
39	otuz toghuz	1000	bir ming
40	qërq	1001	bir ming bir
50	elüü	10,000	on ming
60	altëmësh	100,000	bir jüz ming
70	jetimish	one million	bir miliyon
80	seksen	10 million	on miliyon
90	toqson	100 million	jüz miliyon
100	bir jüz	one billion	bir miliyard
101	bir jüz bir		

EMERGENCIES

Help!	jardam beringiz!
Danger!	qorqunuchtuu!
Don't move!	qëymëldaba (jëlba)!
Stop.	tokto
Go away.	ket
Listen, we're not interested.	qulaq salëngizchë, bul bizge qëziqsiz
Call the police.	milisanë chaqërëngiz
Call a doctor.	dokturdu chaqërëngiz
Could you help me please?	magha jardam berüüingüz düsuraym
There's been an accident.	al jerde qërsëq bolghon
I've been injured.	men jarat aldëm
I've been raped.	meni zorduqtadë
I've been robbed.	meni tonodu
Could I please use the telephone?	men telefon chalëp alsam bolody?
I wish to contact my embassy.	men bizdin elchilikibiz menen baylanëshëm kerek

Kazakh

KAZAKH

INTRODUCTION

Kazakh is spoken by almost 10 million people in nine countries. There are almost seven million Kazakhs living in the huge geographical area that is Kazakhstan; a region of vast steppe lands that is home to the Kazakh nomadic pastoral heritage and lifestyle. The Kazakh language region stretches from the Caspian Sea into the Zhungarian Basin of northwest Xinjiang, China. In the south it comes in contact with the Uzbek, Kyrgyz and Uyghur languages. The Kazakh language most resembles that of the Kyrgyz, who are also nomadic pastoralists. The Kazakh language is also spoken by 1.2 million in Xinjiang, 850,000 in Uzbekistan, 650,000 in Russia; 170,000 in Mongolia, 92,000 in Turkmenistan, 40,000 in Kyrgyzstan and 12,000 in both Ukraine and Tajikistan. Many Kazakhs live as guest workers in Germany.

PRONUNCIATION

The Kazakh language is written in the Cyrillic script in Kazakhstan and a modified Persian-Arabic script in China. As with Kyrgyz, Chinese and Soviet governments imposed changes from a Persian-Arabic script to a Cyrillic or a Roman script in the hope of breaking Kazakhstan's ties to the Muslim world. Kazakh pronunciation is very similar to Kyrgyz (see page 74 for details).

GREETINGS & CIVILITIES

Please.	marhamet
Please sit down.	otur (inf)/oturunguz (pol)
Thank you.	rahmet sizge
Excuse/Pardon me.	kechiringiz
Never mind.	keregi joq (echtem et)
Correct.	tura/durys
Good.	jaqsë
OK.	maqul (jaraidë)

Kazakh Language Area

0   250   500 km

The external boundaries of India on this map have not been authenticated and may not be correct

KAZAKH

KAZAKHSTAN

UZBEKISTAN KYRGYZSTAN

TURKMENISTAN TAJIKISTAN CHINA

IRAN AFGHANISTAN

PAKISTAN

INDIA

RUSSIA

Petropavl

Rudny   Kökshetau   Pavlodar

Oral   Orsk   ✪ Astana   Öskemen

Aqtöbe   Arqalyq   Semey

Karaganda

Atyrau   **KAZAKHSTAN**

Zhezqazghan   Lake Balkash

ARAL SEA

Aqtau   Qyzylorda   Yining   Ürümqi

Almaty

Nukus   Taraz   ✪ Bishkek   **CHINA**

UZBEKISTAN   **KYRGYZSTAN**   (Xinjiang)

Tashkent   Osh   Kashgar

TURKMENISTAN   **TAJIKISTAN**

✪ Ashghabat

Termez

IRAN   **PAKISTAN**   **CHINA**

AFGHANISTAN   **INDIA**   (Tibet)

CASPIAN SEA

KAZAKH

When two friends meet each other, they extend their right hands for a medium firm handshake. While shaking hands, they greet each other by saying salemetsiz be? or qalynyz qalai? This same form of greeting can be observed on the streets, in the workplace and in homes. In social settings it's polite to go around the room greeting everybody with a quick handshake.

There are a few variations to the handshake. If a younger man is greeting an older man, he may show his respect by grasping the older man's hand with both hands. Women or girls who are particularly close sometimes kiss both cheeks while shaking hands. Finally, if a woman who is busy cooking has dirty or wet hands, she extends her right arm with a drooped wrist, thus signalling that the other person should shake her clean wrist rather than her hand.

That will do.	boladë
Do you understand?	tüshindingizbe?
No.	joq
Yes.	iye (sonday)
I understand.	tüsindim
I don't understand.	tüsinbeymin
Sorry.	keshiringiz
No problem.	masele joq
Please wait awhile.	biraz kute tyryngyz
Where's the toilet?	tualet qayjerde?

Greetings & Goodbyes

To end a friendly conversation on the street, you just have to announce that you have something that needs to be done (tilegim bar). If you are visiting someone's house, you are generally expected to stay until you have at least finished many cups of tea, and preferably a hot meal as well. In accordance with the principle of hospitality, Kazakh hosts and hostesses generally discourage their guests from leaving too early. When it's time to leave, you must thank your hosts for their hospitality. Kazakhs usually say goodbye with the phrase sau bolynyz (or the more informal sau bol).

How are you?	salemetsiz be
Peace be upon you.	assalamu alaykim
And upon you be peace.	waghalaykim assalam
How are you?	khalingëz/jagdaiynyz qalai?
Fine (and you?)	jaqsë (sizshi?)
Not bad.	jaman emes
How's your health?	den-sawlëghëngëz qalai?
Have you eaten?	tamaq jedingizbe/tandengezba?
Where are you going?	qayda barasëz?
What are you doing?	ne istep otyrsyz?
Goodbye.	sau bolynyz
See you tomorrow.	erteng koriskenshe
Have a good trip.	sizqe ag jol tileymin
See you soon.	jäne kezdeseimiz
You've been a great help.	siz öte köp komek istedingiz

KAZAKH

LANGUAGE DIFFICULTIES

There are a few sounds that Kazakhs use in place of words. First, there is a low grunt ehhh, that is used to show agreement or to answer 'yes.' Then there is a single click, accompanied by a small shake of the head, which is used to signify 'no.'

Do you speak English?	siz agylshynsha söyley alasez ba?
I don't speak English.	men agylshynsha söyley almaymën
I don't speak Kazakh/Chinese.	men qazaqsha/kitaisha söyley almaymën
Do you have an interpreter?	sizde audarmashëbar ma?
How do you say that in Kazakh?	myna qazaqsha qalai bolodë?
Can you repeat that please?	qaitayap jiberingizshi?
Could you speak louder/ slower please?	qattyraq/asyqpai söyle bolama?
Please point to the word in the book.	mëna kitaptan mëna sözdi körsetip bersengizshi
Let me look in this book.	mena kitaptan izdep köreyin
Just a minute.	qazir, bir minut
What does it mean?	onëng maghanase ne?

KAZAKH

SMALL TALK
Meeting People
There are different standards of behaviour for men and women, even in the cities. Many of these cultural rules vary depending on the situation. When people are around their older relatives and their elders, they act more conservatively.

Women tend to wear conservative clothing but young women who attend university frequently wear jeans and pants. Rural women are expected to wear scarves on their head to indicate that they are married. A young woman is more likely to wear a scarf when she's around her husband's relatives, than around her close friends.

What's your name?	atëngëz kim?
What's your father's name?	ata-anangëzdëng ate kim?
Who are you?	siz kim bolasëz?
I'm happy to see you.	sizben kez deskenisme öte quanështamën
So am I.	mende öte quanështamyn
What time is it?	qazir saghat qansha boldë?
What is this?	byl ne?
Are your parents alive?	ata anangëz bar ma?

Nationalities
Kazakhs are curious about the ethnic identity of travellers. Ethnic identity is an important part of one's identity in the former Soviet Union. And knowledge of one's ancestors is an important part of Kazakh life. So Kazakhs tend to ask foreigners who their ancestors are and whether or not they still know the native language.

What country do you come from?	siz qaysë memleketten keldigniz?
What ethnic group do you come from?	siz qayse ultëgnëz?
I come from (America).	men (amerika)dan keldim

Age
How old are you?	siz qanshä jastasëz?
How old do you think I am?	mini qansha jas dep oylaysëz?
I think you are (35) years old.	siz (otëz bes) jas dep oylaymen

KAZAKH

Religion

I am (a) ...	men ...
Buddhist	butta dini
Catholic	katolik
Christian	khristiyan dini
Hindu	hindu din (hindu)
Jewish	evrei din (evrei)
Muslim	islam dini (musulman)

I'm not religious.   men eshqanday din'ge senbeyminn

Do you attend Mosque?   siz meshitke barasëz ba?
Do you recite daily prayers?   siz namaz oqusyz?

Family

This is ...	bul mening ...
my father/mother	atam/apam
my husband/wife	küyewim/kelinshegim
my girlfriend/boyfriend	jaqsë koreitin qyzym/jigitim
son/daughter	ulëm/qyzym
younger brother/sister	inim/singlim
older brother/sister	agham/apkem
in-law (m)/(f)	quda/qudagi

Are you married? (m)   siz toy jasadyngez ba?
Are you married? (f)   siz tyrmyzga shyqtynyz ba?
I'm married/single.   men uilengenmin/boidaqnyn

How many children do you have?   neshe balagnëz bar?

I don't have any children.   mende bala/balam joq

How many brothers/sisters do you have?   sizding neshe aghaini/apkesinglingiz bar?

I don't have any brothers/sisters.   mening agha-ini/apke-singlim joq

KAZAKH

GETTING AROUND

I'd like to go to ...	men ... barmaqshëmën
How can I get to ...?	men ... nemen bar alamën?
Which (bus) do I take to get to ...?	men qaysë(avtobus) pen ... gha bar alamën?
Is there another way to get there?	basqa amal bar ma?
What time does the next ... leave/arrive?	kelisi ... qashan shygadë/keledi?
bus	avtobus
train	poyëz
plane	samolet/ushaq

Most people on the street are happy to help foreigners with directions. However, many people don't speak English, so some knowledge of Kazakh or Russian is helpful.

Where is the ...?	... qaida/qaisë jerde?
airport	auëjai
bus stop	avtobus ayaldamasë
bus terminal (long-distance)	(uzenjoldë) avtobus voksal
train station	poyez voksalë
ticket office	bilet satatyn kassa

Is it far?	ales pa?
Yes, it's far.	yä, ales
It's quite close.	ol öte jaqen
Can I walk there?	mena jerden jayau jursem bola ma?
How much time will it take to walk there?	jayau jürse qansha waqët ketedi?
What's the address?	adrisi qandai?
Please write down the address for me.	maghan onëng addresin jazëp beringiz
Could you tell the taxi driver the address please?	kire mashëynase (taksi) shoferine bul adrisi aytëp beringiz?
Please draw a map for me.	maghan kharëytasen sëzëp bersengiz

Directions

Which direction?	qaysë baghëtta?
Go straight ahead.	aldëna tüziüjürmekte
Turn right/left.	onggha/solgha burëlëw
direction	baghet
that/this direction	ana/mëna jaq
north/south	soltüstik/ongtüstik
east/west	sheghes/batësh
southeast/northwest	(sheghes ongtüstik)/(batësh soltüstik)
uphill/downhill	taw üsti/bawërë
left/right	sol/ong
at the corner	aynalma
up/down	üsti/tömen
upstairs/downstairs	ustin'gi/astënghe qabat
far away	alës/alësta
inside	ishinde
outside	sërtënda
middle	orta/ortasë
near	jaqën/qasë
near to ...	jaqënda/qasynda

KAZAKH

Buying Tickets

Travellers must pay a special price (in dollars) to travel on planes and trains. These tickets are sold in special windows at the airport and the train station. The price for all buses is the same for foreigners and local travellers.

Where's the ticket office?	bilet satatyn jer qayjerda?
I'd like a (1st class) ticket to (Almaty).	maghan (almaty)gha baraten (birinshi retki)ning bileti kerek
How much is the train to (Karaganda)?	(karaganda)ge baratënnëng bilet baghasë qansha aqsha?
Is there a ticket for the bus to (Almaty) today?	bügün (almaty)gha baratën avtobustëng bileti bar ma?
What is the cheapest fare to (Taraz)?	(taraz)ga eng arzan bilet qaysë?
There are no tickets.	bilet joq

KAZAKH

berth number	orën numuri
cancelled	beker istew
confirm	turaqtandërëw
dormitory bunk	jataq tösegi
first class	birinshi klass bolme
second class	ekinshi (retki) klass
no room	oryn joq
one-way ticket	baru bileti
return tickets	baru-qaitu bileti
refund	aqsha tölewde
seat	oryn
student's ticket	oqëwshëlar bileti
ticket office	bilet satatën orën
timetable	waqët kestesi

Air

A good network of domestic flights link cities all round Kazakhstan and fares are reasonable. The main airlines are Air Astana, a Western-style, Kazakh-British joint venture; and SCAT, a Kazakh airline flying prop-driven Russian planes.

This price is higher than normal.	bul bagha ädettegiden jogharë
aeroplane	samolet/ushaq
airline ticket	samolet bilet
customs' (declaration)	tamujna (mälimeti)
departure	ayërëlu
estimated time of arrival/ departure	keletin/ketetin vaqyttyn jobasë
gate number	esik numuri
no smoking	temeki shegiwge bolmayde
passport	passport

Bus

All cities in Kazakhstan have buses and trolley-buses. These are very inexpensive but they are also slow and often very crowded. It's custom-ary for everybody to pass forward the appropriate fare as soon as they get on the bus. This means that there is a regular flow of money toward the front of the bus and a flow of receipts towards the back of the bus.

Is this going to the (bazaar)?	ol (bazaar)gha barama?
I want to get off at ...	mën ... de tusemin
Please tell me when we've reached that stop.	ol ayaldamaga qashan baratëndëghën maghan aytëp beringizshi
bus (terminal)	avtobus(deng voksalë)
long-distance bus station	uzën joldë avtobus voksalë

KAZAKH

Train

Newer trains have air-conditioning that works, and are spacious and clean. Train passengers generally bring their own food. However, at certain stops along the way, merchants walk through the train selling beer, food and candy bars. Women travelling alone should ask the conductor (provodnik) to put them in a coupee with other women or with a family. Baggage compartments within a coupee are often very crowded.

Can you help me find my seat/berth please?	ornymë tawepalëlwem üchün jardem beringizshi?
Excuse me, this is my seat.	keshiringiz bul mening ornum
Where's the dining car?	poyez askhanasë qayjerda?
common wagon (no beds)	jalpëvagon
dining car	poyez askhanasë
(express/fast) train	(ekspress/jurdek) poyez

Taxi

Taxis or private cars can be easily hailed within a few minutes on any busy street. You should agree on a price before getting into the car. Private cars do not have meters, but there's always a commonly accepted rate per kilometre, which changes constantly with the changing price of fuel. While all drivers know this rate, some try to charge a higher rate, especially with foreigners.

I'd like to go to ...	mën ... gha barmaqshëmën
How long does it take to go to ...?	... ke barew üshün qanshalëq waqët ketedi?
Are any English-speaking drivers available?	agylshynsha soyley alaten shofer barma?

KAZAKH

How much?	qansha aqsha?
Please stop here.	ose jerde tyryngyz
Stop at the next corner.	jäne bir byryshda toqtangez
Please hurry.	tezirek bolëngëz
Please slow down.	qarqëndë bayawtatëngëz
Please wait here.	ose jerde tosëngëz
I'll get off here.	men ose jerde tusemin
Where can I hire a taxi?	qayjerden täksi jalda alamyn?
How much is it for one/ three day(s)?	bir/üsh kündigi aqshasë qansha?

Useful Words

accident	avariya
air-conditioning	konditsioner
battery	batariya (elektir mayë)
(rent a) bicycle	velosiped (jaldau)
brake	tormëz
car	mashëyna
engine oil	maslo
fill up	toltru
flat tyre	razenke dönggelek
headlight	aldën ghësham
highway	jogharë qarqëndë tas jol
(international) driving licence	(khalyqaralyq) shoferlik pravasë
map	karta
motorbike	motosikl
parking	toqtatëu
petrol	benzin
radiator	radiator
service station	sawda orenë
taxi stand	täksine jaldau
tyre	dönggelek

ACCOMMODATION

It's fairly common for foreigners to stay with local families. While there are some organisations which arrange homestays, it's possible to make your own arrangements with somebody that you trust.

Kazakhs pride themselves on their hospitality and most families could use the extra income. Negotiating prices can be awkward though because many Kazakhs don't like to profit from guests. One solution is to provide gifts instead of cash.

If you go to somebody's house for dinner or tea, it is nice to bring some sort of food item, such as fresh fruits or imported cookies. If there are any children in the house, it is nice to bring them something separate, such as a chocolate bar or a small toy.

hotel	mëymankhana	dormitory	jataqkhana
inn	qonaq üy	guesthouse	qonaq üy
apartment	nater, kvartira	youth hostel	jashtar qonaq üy

Where's a guesthouse? — qonaq üy qayjërde?

I'm looking for a ... hotel. — men ... qonaq üy izdeymin
   cheap — arzan
   clean — taza
   good — jaqsë
   near-the-city — qalaneng mangëndaghë
   near-the-airport — auëalangënëng mangendghë
   nearby — jaqën jerden

Booking a Room

Do you have any rooms available? — bos bolme bar ma?

Do you have any beds available? — bos tösek bar ma?

I would like a ... — maghan bir ... kerek
   single/twin room — jalghez/eki kisilik bolme
   quiet room — tënësh bolme
   big room — ülken bolme
   (double) bed — (iki kisilik) tosek

At the Hotel

How much is it per night/ person? — bir keshe/kisilik qansha aqsha?

Is there a discount for students/ children? — oqëwchegha/balalargha baghada kongil bolineme?

KAZAKH

Can I get a discount if I stay longer?	uzaq tursam baghada kongil böesizbe?
Are there any cheaper ones?	arzanëraghnan bireri bar ma?
Can I see the room first?	aldëmën bolmeni körsem bola ma?
Are there any others?	basqasë bar ma?
It's fine, I'll take this room.	bul boladëeken, men osëbolmeni alayen
I'm going to stay for ...	men ... turmaqshëmën
one/two night(s)	bir/iki tün
a few days	birneshe kün
a week	bir apta
Can I have the key please?	kiltti maghan beresizbe?
Is hot water available all day?	ësteq suw ünemi barma?
Could I have a different room?	basqä bolme alsam bola ma?
Any messages for me?	maghan khabare bar ma?
Please do not disturb.	ëqpal jetkizbengizshi

KAZAKH

Requests & Complaints

It's too ...	bul öte ...
big/small	ulken/kishkene
cold/hot	suwyq/ëstyq
dark/dirty	qarangghe/kir
noisy	ayghay (shuw)

It smells.	bul iyistenip qalëptë
The toilet/sink is blocked.	daretkhana/juëndëturba bitelip qalëptë
The door is locked.	esik bekitilip qalëptë
My room number is (123).	bolme nomirim (bir jüz jëyërma üsh)
Please fix it as soon as possible.	mënanëtezirek orantep bersengizshi

Checking Out

I'd like to check out now/tomorrow.	(men) esep jasamaqchëmën qazir/erteng
I'd like to pay the bill.	men schyotgha aqsha tölemekshimin
Can I leave my bags here for a few days?	men jukterimdi bul jerde birneshe kün qoyep tursam bola ma?
Thank you for your hospitality.	mëymandostëghynyzga rahmet

I am returning ...	men ... qaytamën
tomorrow	erteng
in 2-3 days	ekiüsh künde
next week	kelesi apta

Useful Words

address	ädiris	bed	tosek
baggage	sumka/juk	bill	schyot
balcony	balkon	blanket	ädiyal
basin	dos	bucket	shelek
bathroom	monshakhana	door	esik

KAZAKH

key	kilt	lock	zamok/bekitkish
laundry	kir juatyn üy	luggage	juk
lift (elevator)	lift	room	bolme
light bulb	lampushkha	shower	dush
lobby	karidor	toilet	tualet

AROUND TOWN

In Kazakh cities, the main administration buildings and cultural buildings are in the centre of town. Nearby, there are usually spacious parks with benches. Young people of all nationalities spend a lot of time gathering with their friends in the parks.

At the Bank

account	esep
amount	esep somasë
buying rate	setiwelish närgi
cash	näh pul
cashier	kassir
cheque	shek/aqsha segi
credit card	bedeldi qart
deposit	amanat
exchange (rate)	ayerbas (baghasë)
foreign currency	shetel aqshasë
money exchange	aqsha ayërbastaw
official rate	ökimet narqë
receipt	khujat
signature	kol (qoyëw)
travellers' cheque	sayahat shegi
withdrawal	qaytereptastaw

At the Post Office

Despite a bad reputation, the postal service in Kazakhstan is fairly reliable. It takes anywhere from two to three weeks for a letter to arrive from the USA. Both Kazakh and Russian are spoken, and international parcels can only be mailed from the central post office.

I'd like to send ... to (Australia).	men ... (austriläya)gha jibergim keledi
How much is it?	bul qansha aqsha?
How much does this weigh?	buneng awërlëghë qansha?

address	adris	post code	poshta nomiri
aerogram	sëmsëz telegraf	poste restante	do vostrebovaniya
airmail	jedel pochta	post office	pochta
envelope	konvert	registered mail	zakaz khat
fax	faks	stamps	marka
insurance	qamsëzdandëru	surface mail	ädettegi khat
letter	khat	(urgent)	(shughyl)
parcel	posylka	telegram	telegramma
postcard	otkrytka		

KAZAKH

Telephone

I want to make a phone call to (Canada).	men (kanada)gha telefon soggym keledi
What's the number?	telefon nomiri qansha?
The number is ...	telefon nomiri ...
Hello.	wäy
Can I speak to ...?	mën ... menen soyleidëbola ma?

collect call	baskëkisi toleidi
country code	memliket nomiri
directory	telefon (nomiri) däpteri
engaged	(telefon) seme bos emes
international call	khalyqaraleq telefon
public telephone	ünemi istetiletin telefon
telephone (number)	telefon (nomiri)
wrong number	qata nomir

Sightseeing

What's the name of this place?	bul järdin ati ne?
Excuse me, what's this/that?	kechiringiz, bul/ol ne?
Do you have a (local) map?	sizde (jerlik) kharyta barma?
Am I allowed to take photos here?	bul jerde suret tusiruge bola ma?
What time does it open/close?	(bul) qashan ashëladë/ jabyladë?

KAZAKH

How much is the ...?	... qansha aqsha?
admission fee	belet baghasë
guidebook	sayakhat aqnar-kitapsha
postcard	otkrytka

Useful Words

ancient	ejelgi	museum	muzei
archaeology	arkheologiya	old city	äski kala
building	gimarat	ruins	köni eskimish
exhibition	korme	sculpture	skulptura
monument	eskertkish	souvenirs	estelik buyëmë

IN THE COUNTRY

The natural beauty of the steppe land in central and southern Kazakhstan includes many herds of sheep, horses and camels. Some of the most beautiful areas of Kazakhstan include the lakes around Kokshetau in the north and the mountains near Almaty in the south. To tell somebody that you want to look around their village, you say;

men aulynyzdy qydyryp zhurgym keledi

Weather

What's the weather like today/ tomorrow?	bügün/erteng awaraye qanday?
The weather's nice today.	bügün awaraye jaqsë
Will it rain tomorrow?	erteng jangber jawa ma?
It's hot.	ëstëq
It's raining.	jangber jawep jatër

It's ...	awa ...
fine	jaqsë
clear/cloudy	bulëttë
dark/sunny	qarangghë/nurlë
very cold/hot	öte suwëq/ëstëq

Along the Way

When do we go?	qashan jolgha shëghamëz?
Where are we?	biz qayjerde?

Can you please tell me how to get to ...?
...ge qanday boratenen aytep beresizbe?

What will we pass on the way?
biz jolda qays jerlerden ötemiz?

How far is it from here to ...?
bul jerden ...ge deyin araleghe qansha?

Are there any things to see here/there?
bul jerde köriwge tiyisti ne narseler bar?

Let's take a rest here.
bul jerde dem alayeq

Can I have a cup of water/tea?
bir istakan suw/shäy barma?

KAZAKH

Seasons

spring	köktem	autumn	küz
summer	jaz	winter	qës
cave	ünggür	mountain range	tawlërayon
country	qër (uwël)		
desert	qumdë	mountain (trail)	taw (jolë)
earth	dünya		
earthquake	jer silkiniw	public toilet	alwmettik daretkhana
farm	auëlsharuashëlyq maydanë		
		river	özen
high plateau	biyiktik	road	jol
hill	döng	rock	tas
hot springs	arasan	seasons	mawsemdar
lake	köl	valley	anggar
landslide	taw qulaw	village	awel
map	karta	well	qudëq

Animals

Many people keep dogs as guard dogs, rather than as pets, and some can be fairly vicious. Travellers also need to be careful around horses.

cat	mysyq	monkey	maimyl
dog	it	mouse	tyshqan
donkey	eshak	sheep	qoy
horse	at		

KAZAKH

FOOD

When Kazakhs invite guests for dinner, they cover the table with food. Kazakhs living in the cities tend to eat at tall European tables, while Kazakhs in villages tend to eat their meals while sitting on the floor.

When guests arrive, they are directed to seats in the place of honour which is the area farthest from the entrance. The father of the household will sit near the guest, while women will sit closer to the door so that they can easily go to the kitchen for food and tea. When men sit on the floor, it is appropriate to sit with legs crossed. Women should sit by kneeling on their legs or with legs to one side.

Beshparmaq is considered to be the national dish of Kazakhstan. It involves boiled mutton served on top of wide, noodles. When guests are present, a meal of beshparmaq usually begins with the presentation of a blackened sheep head to the male guest of honour. The guest is expected to slice pieces of the sheep head for himself and others, before passing the plate to somebody else. Beshparmaq is traditionally eaten with one's right hand, although some families might provide a foreign guest with a fork and separate plate.

bar	bar
market	dükän
restaurant	resturan
tea house	shaykhana

I want to go to a restaurant restaurant with Kazakh/ Chinese food.	men qazaq/kitai tamaghe men restoran'gha baramën

At the Restaurant

Can I see the menu please?	tamaq tizimdigi däpterin koruge bola ma?
I'd like what he's eating.	bul adamning jägän tamaghinday jägim kälidi
Do you have an English menu?	agëlshënsha tamaq tizimdigi bar ma?
Can you recommend any dishes?	qanday jaqsë tamaq tarëngez bar?
Do you have a knife and fork?	peshaq pen wekangëz bar ma?
The bill please.	schyot jasangëzshë
I don't eat meat.	et jemeymin

I would like to have ...   men ... ala laymen
  alcoholic drinks   araq
  beverages   susyndar
  food   tamagh
  noodles   kespe
  pilaf   palau
  rice   kurish

göshnan (etnan)	nan bread with mutton
koje/sorpa	mutton soup with noodle flakes
lagman	spaghetti-like pulled noodles

KAZAKH

Breakfast, Lunch & Dinner

breakfast	azangghi tamagh	milk	süt
dinner	käshki tamagh	snack	qosëmsha tamagh
eggs	jomurtqa	tea	shäy
flat bread	nan	yoghurt	ayran
lunch	tüskü tamagh		

SHOPPING

Bazaars offer a lot of interesting sights, smells and tastes. In the meat section, it's possible to buy a sheep head or a horse head. Kazakhs present these heads to their guests as a sign of respect. You might want to try kumiss (horse's milk) or komyran (camel's milk) or, in the Almaty bazaar, the spicy Korean salads sold by the local Korean population.

How many?	qansha?
How much?	baghase qansha?
I'd like to buy ...	men ... alamaqshëmën
I'm just looking.	men tek körip otyrmyn
How much does this/that cost?	menaw/anaw qansha aqsha?
That's very expensive.	anaw qëmbat eken
That's cheap.	ol qimbat emes
Can you reduce the price?	baghasën biraz tüsirip beresiz be?
Where can I buy a ...?	men ... ne qayjerden al alaymen?

KAZAKH

Where's the nearest ...?	eng jaqendaghë ... qayjerde?
bazaar	bazaar
grocery store	azyq-tulik dukeni
store	magazin/duken
pharmacy	därikhana

Sizes & Quantities

a bottle/container of	bir butylka
dozen	dyujina
half a dozen	jartä dyujina
one metre	bir mätr
two kilometres	iki kilomätr
one metre/litre	bir mätr/litr

Colours

black	qara	red	qizil
blue	kök	white	aq
green	jasyl	yellow	sare

HEALTH

The education level of doctors in Kazakhstan is much higher than the services they are able to provide. Many hospitals lack basic supplies and medicines. Hospitals in the villages do not even have indoor plumbing. Many doctors in Kazakhstan, though, have received adequate medical training, either in Almaty or in Moscow.

I'm sick.	men awërëwmën
My friend is sick.	dosëm awerew
I need a doctor.	men darigerge körinemin
I need a doctor who can speak English.	maghan agylshynsha söyley alaten dariger kerek
I want a doctor that practises western/Chinese medicine.	maghan batëssha/kitaisha dawalaytën dariger kerek
Can you bring a doctor to my room?	jataghema bir dariger ertip kelsengez?
Please take me to a doctor.	meni darigerge aparsangez
I've been injured.	men jaralandim

KAZAKH

I need an ambulance.	maghan tez qutqarew mashëynasë kerek
Can you tell me where the ... is?	maghan ... qaysë jerde ekenim aytëp berealasëzba?
clinic	klinika/emkhana
doctor	dariger
hospital	aurukhana
nurse	medsestra
pharmacy	därikhana
I need an English interpreter.	maghan bir agylshynsha audarmashë kerek
I want a female doctor.	maghan bir äyel dariger kerek
Please use a new syringe.	jana shprits istetsengizshi
I have my own syringe.	özimning shpritisim bar
I don't want a blood transfusion.	men qanym döbermemin
I am not feeling well.	densawlëghëm joq
How long before it will get better?	jazëlëwëna qansha waqët ketedi?

THE DOCTOR MAY SAY ...

ne bolde?	What's wrong?
qayjeringiz awërëptur?	Where does it hurt?
qandayëraq?	How are you feeling?
awërëp jaterma?	Do you feel any pain?
qëzëp jatërsëzba?	Do you have a temperature?
buren qanday awërëwëngëz bolgan?	What illnesses have you had in the past?
temeki shegesiz be?	Do you smoke?
araq ishesiz be?	Do you drink?
ekiqabattësëz ba?	Are you pregnant?
kününä (bir) mäzgil (tort) danadan däraalu	Take (1) tablet (4) times a day.

KAZAKH

Parts of the Body

arm	bilek	heart	jürek
bone	süyek	kidney	büyrek
breast	ëmshëq	leg	sëyraq/ayaq
ear	qulaq	lung	ökpe
eye	köz	mouth	awez
face	bet	pulse	qan tamër
finger	barmaq	skin	teri
foot	ayaq	stomach	asqazan
hand	qol	throat	tamaq
head	bas	urine	sidik

Ailments

I ...
men ...

have an insect bite
qurt-qumyrsqa qabuë

can't move my ...
... qozghalta almaymën

can't sleep
uyeqtay almaymën

lost my appetite
konglim tartpayde

have missed my period
for ... months
... ay esimdi joqhaltep
aldëm

am pregnant
ekiqabattymyn

vomited
qusëp tastadem (qustëm)

am weak
älsiz

I have ...
mening ...

altitude sickness
qobalju

asthma
demikpe/astma

a cold/influenza
tumaw

constipation
ish jurmen

diabetes
diabet

diarrhoea
ich ötiw

dizziness
base aynalëw

a fever
qezew

have a heart condition
jürigim shanship jatir

hepatitis
bawër awërëwë/gepatit

an itch
qyshu

lice
bit

KAZAKH

a migraine	turup (bas) awërëw
a stomachache	ish awërëw
venereal disease	jënës awërëwë
I'm allergic to (antibiotics).	men (baktiriyagha qarsë) aurughumän awiridim

At the Chemist

May I have ... please?	(maghan) ... bor ma?
aspirin	aspirin
Band-Aids	sipidi
condoms	prezervativ
cough remedy	tumaw därisi
eyedrops	köz därisi
insect repellent	qurtqa qarsë därisi
painkiller	awërëw basatendäri
sanitary napkins	gigiyencheskie prokladki
sleeping pills	tënështandërëw därisi
contraceptive pills	iki qabattylyqa qarsë därisi
travel sickness pills	tënështandërëw därisi

At the Dentist

dentist	tis dariger
tooth/teeth	tis/tister
toothache	tis awërëwë
wisdom tooth	aqyl tis
Is there a dentist here?	bul jerde tis darigeri bar ma?
I don't want it extracted.	men tisisindi juldërtpaymën
Please give me an anaesthetic.	meni töksirudän otkizsingiz

Useful Words

accident	apat	blood pressure	qan basëmë
acupuncture	ighlatirafiya	contraceptive	prezervativ
AIDS	SPID	eye (drops)	köz
antibiotic	antibiotik		(qarchëghasë)
antiseptic	antisäptik	first aid	tez qutqarew
blood	qan	glasses	közeynek
(group/test)	(tiyipi/tekseriw)	injection	okil qoyëw

KAZAKH

menstruation	ay köriw	surgeon	sërtgëawëlëlar
optometrist	optika		derigeri/khirurg
pneumonia	ökpe	syringe	sepkish
	qabënëw	virus	virus
Red Cross	qëzël kires	vitamin	vetämin
specialist	käsiptik	X-ray	rentin nure
	dariger		

TIME, DATES & FESTIVALS
Telling the Time

When?	qashan?
What time is it?	hazir saghat qansha (boldë)?
At what time?	saghat qanshada?

hour	saghat	afternoon	tusten keyin
... o'clock	saghat ...	noon	tüs
half past ...	... jarëm	evening	kesh
a quarter	sherik	midnight	jarem tün
morning	tängërtëng		

Days of the Week

Sunday	jeksenbi	Thursday	beysenbi
Monday	düysenbi	Friday	juma
Tuesday	seysenbi	Saturday	senbi
Wednesday	särsenbi		

Months

January	yaneyar/qangtar	July	iyul/shilde
February	febiral/aqpan	August	awghust/tamez
March	mart/nawërëz	September	sentabir/qerküyek
April	aprel/kökek	October	öktabir/qazan
May	may/mamër	November	noyabir/qarasha
June	iyun/mawsëm	December	dekabir/jeltoqsan

Present, Past & Future

today	bugun	(this) month	(bul) ay
tonight	keshte	yesterday	keshe
(this) week	(bul) apta	last week	otken apta

last month	ötken ay	next week	keler apta
tomorrow	erteng	next month	keler ay

Festivals & Holidays

Kazakhstan is still in the midst of discarding old Soviet holidays and creating new Kazakhstan ones. As a result, there are a number of holidays that are observed, but many are no longer official.

The most popular public holidays are New Year's jangëjël and naurëz (Persian-Central Asian New Year's). New Year's is celebrated both at work and at home. Small presents are exchanged and people celebrate at home with their friends and relatives.

During naurëz, a large festival is held on the streets of every city and town. Traditional Kazakh songs and dances are performed in the streets. Various public and private organisations set up dozens of yurts along the main streets which have food and drinks.

Ramadan is observed at a different time every year, according to the lunar calendar. Kazakhs celebrate the end of Ramadan, oraza ait, by visiting the homes of their closest friends and relatives and eating special foods.

January 1 jangëjël – New Years
January 7 – Orthodox Christmas
March 8 – International Women's Day
Oraza Ait – Festival marking the end of Ramadan fast
March 21 nawerez merekesi – Persian New Year, Spring Festival
May 9 – Veteran's Day/WW II Memorial Day
qurban ait – Festival celebrating Abraham's attempted sacrifice of
      his son and is the day when Muslims make their hajj to Mecca
December 16 – Independence Day
memileket merekesi – National Day

NUMBERS

0	nöl	5	bes	10	on	15	on bes
1	bir	6	altë	11	on bir	16	on alte
2	iki	7	jeti	12	on eki	17	on jeti
3	üsh	8	segiz	13	on üsh	18	on segiz
4	tort	9	toghez	14	on tort	19	on toghëz

KAZAKH

KAZAKH

20	jëyërma	110	bir jüz on
21	jëyërma bir	115	bir jüz on bes
22	jëyërma eki	120	bir jüz jëyërma
23	jëyërma üsh	190	bir jüz toqsan
30	otez	200	eki jüz
39	otez toghëz	1000	bir mëng
40	qërëq	1001	bir mëng bir
50	eliw	10,000	on mëng
60	alpes	100,000	bir jüz mëng
70	jetpis	one million	bir milyon
80	seksen	10 million	on milyon
90	toqsan	100 million	jüz milyon
100	jüz	one billion	bir milyard
101	bir jüz bir		

EMERGENCIES

Help!	täshindir!
Danger!	kaup!
Don't move!	qozghama!
Stop.	tokhta
Go away.	shiq
Listen, we're not interested.	tingda, biz qiziqbaybiz
Call the police.	militsia shaqirshi
Call a doctor.	dariger shaqirshi
Could you help me please?	maghan jardäm bäringizshä?
There's been an accident.	ol järdäbir apat boldi
I've been injured.	men ukol alanmin
I've been raped.	bireu meni zorladë
I've been robbed.	meni tonap kätti
Could I please use the telephone?	men tëlëfondi alamën ba?
I wish to contact my embassy.	men yëlshilikpën baylanisayin

Pashto

PASHTO

INTRODUCTION

Pashto (known as Pakhto in Pakistan) is an Indo-European language spoken in Pakistan and Afghanistan by the over 30 million people known as Pathans. Pathans, in their own language, are known as Pakhtuns in Pakistan and Pashtoons in Afghanistan. In this book we have referred to the people as Pashtoons and the language as Pashto. Pashto is the native language of the 18.5 million Pakistanis living in Northwest Frontier province, and of groups in Beluchistan and in the Pakistan capital Karachi. Pashto is also a national language of Afghanistan, spoken by 12 million people who make up the majority of the Afghan population. Pashto is spoken outside Central Asia by over 165,000 Pathans living in the United Arab Emirates, over 70,000 in Iran, and 90,000 in the UK.

PRONUNCIATION

The Pashto language is written in an Arabic script. Most Pashto sounds are also found in the English language, while a few additional ones must be learned. Intonation is important and this can be learned quickly by listening to Pashtoons speak.

Vowels

There are 10 vowels in the Pashto language and almost all correspond to English sounds, except the elongated sounds indicated by double vowels aa, ee, and oo.

a	as in 'father'
ai	soft 'e' sound as in 'set'
aa	as a long 'ah' sound stretched with a glottal stop
e	as the 'oo' sound in 'good'
ee	as a long 'oo' sound as in 'mm, mm gooood!'
ei	as the 'ay' in 'day'
i	as in 'bill'
o	as in 'go'
oo	as a stretched 'oh' sound
u	as in 'put'

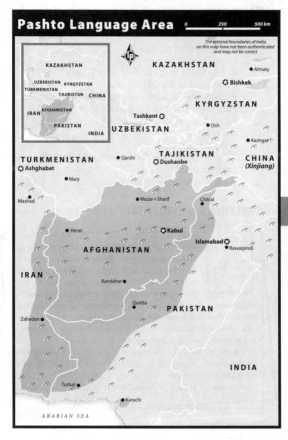

Pashto Language Area

0   250   500 km

The external boundaries of India on this map have not been authenticated and may not be correct

KAZAKHSTAN

● Almaty

✪ Bishkek

KYRGYZSTAN

✪ Tashkent   ● Osh

● Kashgar

UZBEKISTAN

TAJIKISTAN   CHINA
(Xinjiang)

● Qarshi   ✪ Dushanbe

TURKMENISTAN

✪ Ashghabat   ● Mary

● Mashad   ● Mazar-i-Sharif   Chitral

● Herat   ✪ Kabul

AFGHANISTAN   Islamabad ✪
● Rawalpindi

IRAN

Kandahar ●

Quetta ●   PAKISTAN

● Zahedan

INDIA

● Turbat   ● Karachi

ARABIAN SEA

Inset map:

KAZAKHSTAN

UZBEKISTAN   KYRGYZSTAN

TURKMENISTAN   TAJIKISTAN   CHINA

AFGHANISTAN

IRAN   PAKISTAN

INDIA

PASHTO

Consonants

h	with aspiration as in 'haste', but silent at the end of a word
j	as in 'jar'
p	slightly muffled as in 'push'
q	a hard 'k' as in the Arab country 'Qatar'
r	slightly trilled, soft, and close to an 'l' sound
ch	pronounced as the 'ch' in 'cheek'
gh	similar to the French 'r' (see page16 for an explanation)
kh	a soft rasped 'ch' sound as in the Scottish 'loch'
KH	the hard rasped 'ch' sound in the Yiddish 'chutzpah'
ng	as the 'ng' in 'rung.'
sh	as the 'sh' in 'sheep.'
th	a 't' pronounced with the tongue behind the front teeth, barely aspirated
zh	as the 's' in 'vision' and 'treasure'

PASHTO

GREETINGS & CIVILITIES

Men hug after not seeing each other for a long time. They hug three times placing their head on either shoulder. Then they will use both hands to shake each other's hands. Upon meeting for the first time only the two-handed shake is used. When family members meet they will kiss one another on the cheek. When men greet women they don't touch. Afghans greet one another by placing their right hand on the heart and bowing slightly. Doing this indicates that one is an Afghan.

It's proper for a female tourists to kiss a Pashtoon woman on the cheeks. In greeting an older woman it's very polite and endearing for a woman, even foreigners, to kiss her hand. For foreign men, it's a sign of respect to kiss an older man's hand.

Please (sit down).	lutfan (kena)
Thank you.	sta na shukria

Excuse/Pardon me.	bakhena ghuarum
Never mind.	parwa ne lary
Correct.	sum
Good.	KHe
OK.	hoo/sama da
That will do.	wo ba shi
Do you understand?	poh shwey?
No.	na
Yes.	hoo
I (don't) understand.	ze (ne) pohigam
Sorry.	wobakha
No problem.	parwa neshta
Please wait awhile.	lutfan lag saber waka
Where's the toilet?	tashnab cherta day?

PASHTO

To indicate 'yes' the head is moved forward and back. To indicate 'what?' or 'pardon' the head is moved backwards one or two times. To indicate that something is very far a Pashtun extends the hand palmside up, making a backslash at head level, and raises the voice when saying 'far.' A click sound with an outward circular hand movement indicates 'don't mention it' or 'it's not important'.

Greetings & Goodbyes

Good morning/day/evening.	assalam u alaikum
	(lit: peace be upon you)
And upon you peace.	wa alaikum u ssalam
Good night.	shpa dey pe khair
How are you?	tha tsanga yei?
Fine.	KHe
Fine, and you?	ze khe yem aw ta?
Not bad.	bad na yem
How is your health?	sehat de tsanga dai?
Have you eaten?	dooday de kwaraly da?
Where are you going?	chertha zey?
What are you doing?	tsa kawey?
I'm fine.	ze KHe yem

When saying goodbye both hands are used to shake hands fervently
and you should smile.

Goodbye.	de kuday pe aman
See you tomorrow.	saba ba sarra wowino
Have a good trip.	saffar dey pe khair
See you soon.	sta de zer lidu pe hila
You've been a great help.	stha le mrastey shukria

LANGUAGE DIFFICULTIES

Do you speak English?	ta pe angrezai pohegy?
I don't speak Pashto/Urdu.	ze pe pashto/urdu ne pohigam
Do you have an interpreter?	ta tarjuman larey?
How do you say that in Pashto?	dey ta pe pakhto ke tsa wayee?
Can you repeat that please?	lutfan da tekrar ka?
Could you speak louder/ slower please?	lutfan pe lwar/teet awaz khabery waka?
Please point to the word/ phrase in the book.	lutfan dagha jumla/lughat pe ketab ke paida ka
Just a minute.	lag saber
What does it mean?	da tsa mana larie?

SMALL TALK
Meeting People

What's your name?	sta noom tse day?
What's your father's name?	stha de plar noom tse day?
Who are you?	tha tsook ye?
I'm pleased to meet you.	sta pe lidelo khuakh shoom
So am I.	ze hum khuakh shoom
What time is it?	tso bajey dee?
What's this?	dha tse shay day?
Are your parents alive?	stha plar zhwandee dhee?
My (mother) is alive but my (father) is not.	zema (moor) zhwanday da kho (plar) mey neshta

Nationalities

What country do you come from?	tha la kuom hiwad na raghelay yee?
What ethnic group do you come from?	tha da kuomy qabiley yee?
I come from (the USA).	za la (amriky) na raghelay yem

Age

How old are you?	tha tso kalan yee?
How old do you think I am?	stha pa khial tso kalan yem?
I think you are (35) years old.	zema pa khial (penze dersh) kalan yee

Religion

It's better not to tell older people that you're not religious, especially if they are Muslim.

PASHTO

I'm (a) ...	za aqida larem pa ...
Buddhist	budaee din
Catholic	katolik
Christian	eisaee
Confucianism	kanfusi din
Hindu	hindu din
Jewish	yehudi din
Muslim	islam

I'm not religious.	za maz habee na yem
Do you attend Mosque?	tha jumat ta zey?
I attend Mosque every Friday.	ze hara juma jumat ta zem

Family

This is my ...	da dai zema ...
father/mother	plar/more
husband	khawend/tsakhten
wife	mermen/kheza
boyfriend/girlfriend	namzad/namzada
son/daughter	zoi/loor
younger brother/sister	kesher wroor/khoor
older brother/sister	mesher wroor/khoor

Are you married?	ta wada keray dai?
I'm married.	ma wada keray dai
I'm single.	ze mujarad yem
How many children do you have?	tso auladona larey?
I don't have any children.	ze aulad ne larem
How many brothers/sisters do you have?	tso wrona/khuaindei larey?
I don't have any brothers/sisters.	ze wroor/khoor ne larem.

GETTING AROUND

I'd like to go to ...	ze ghuaram che ... ta lar shem
How can I get to ...?	tsenge ba ... ta warasegam?
Which (bus) do I take to get to ...?	pe kuom (bus) ke ba ... ta lar shem?
Is there another way to get there?	dagha zai ta bela lar sheta?

What time does the next ... leave/arrive?	bal ba pe tso bajo ... rarasigi/rawanigi?
bus	bus
train	trayn
plane	jaz

Pashtoons are reliable when it comes to giving directions to tourists. They'll let you know if they don't know the location desired.

Where is the ...?	cherta dai ...?
airport	hawaie dagar
bus stop	tamzai
bus terminal	bus ada
train station	railway stashun
ticket office	tiket dafter

Is it far?	da lirey dai?
Yes, it's far.	ho da liray dai
It's quite close.	deyr land dai
Can I walk there?	pe pakho telalai shem?

PASHTO

How much time will it take to walk there?	pe pakho warta tsomra wakht pe kar dai?
What's the address?	pata ye tsa da?
Please write down the address for me.	lutfan mata pata walika
Could you tell the taxi driver the address please?	mehrabani waka da taxi driwer ta pata wowaya?
Please draw a map for me.	mata naqsha wobasa

Directions

Which direction?	pe kum taraf dai?
this/that direction	da/hagha taraf
Go straight ahead.	negh lar sha
Turn right/left.	khai/chap taraf ta wagarza
direction	taraf
north/south	shimal/janub
east/west	sharq/gharb
southeast	janub sharq
northwest	shimal gharb
uphill	makh parta
downhill	makh khekata
left/right	chap/KHai
at the corner	korner
up/down	porta/koozs
upstairs/downstairs	porta/kooz manzel
far away	deyr lirey
outside	bahar
inside	pe manz ke
middle	manzanai
near (to ...)	(... ta) negdey

PASHTO

Buying Tickets

Where's the ticket office?	the tiketono dafter cherta dai?
I'd like a (first class) ticket to (Lahore).	ghuarum che (first klas) tiket (lahore) ta wakhlem

How much is the train to (Peshawar)?	(peshawar) ta da rail tiket pa tso dai?
Is there a ticket for the bus to (Islamabad) today?	(islamabad) to nan da bus tiket paida kegy?
What's the cheapest fare to (Lahore)?	(lahore) ta arzana keraya tso da?
There are no tickets.	tiketona neshta

berth number	da kat lumber
berth upper/lower	da khobe kat portanai/khekatanai
cancelled	kansel
confirm	kanfirm
dormitory bunk	kut
economy class	teta daraja
1st class	lomrai daraja
2nd class	duaiama daraja
one-way ticket	yau tarafa tiket
return tickets	wapasi tiket
refund	bert akhestel
seat	chawkai/seat
student's ticket	mutalim tiket
ticket office	tiketono dafter
timetable	taqsim auqat

Air

I want to confirm my flight.	ghuarum khpel tiket konfirm kem
This price is higher than normal.	da bia deyra ochata da

aeroplane	jaz
airline ticket	jaz tiket
customs	gumrak
customs' declaration	gumraky elan
departure	harakat
estimated time of arrival/ departure	the rarasedelo/harakat wakht

PASHTO

gate number	the darwazey lamber
no smoking	sigret mam now
passport	pasport

Bus

Long-distance buses leave from the central station. Buses, 'flying coaches', are brightly painted and have music as well as video monitors showing Pakistani love stories.

Is this going to the (bazaar)?
 da (bazar) ta zi?

I want to get off at ...
 ze ghuaram pe ... ke kooz shem

Please tell me when we've reached that stop.
 hagha stap ta pe rasedo me khabar ka

bus (terminal)	bus (adda)
long-distance bus station	loya adda

Train

There are 1st- and 2nd-class sleeper cars which can have four people per compartment. In the regular 1st class there are 20 passengers and in 2nd class there are over one hundred.

Can you help me find my seat/berth please?	mehrabani waka mata seat/kut paida ka?

Excuse me, this is my seat.	bakhena ghuarum da zema sea dai
Where's the dining car?	the restaran dabba cherta da?
dining car	de restaran dabba
express/fast train	tez raw/gam trayn
hard seat (2nd class)	de largy seat (duaiema daraja)
hard-sleeper (2nd class)	de largy kut (duaiema daraja)
soft-seat (1st class)	aram seat (first klas)
train	trayn/orgaday

Taxi

To flag down a taxi you stick out your hand as if shaking hands. It's essential to negotiate the price before getting into the cab and only a very small tip is needed. It's best for women to ride in the front seat with men in the back.

I'd like to go to ...	ze ghuarum che ... ta lar shem
How long does it take to go to ...?	... ta tsomra lar da?
Are any English-speaking drivers available?	pe angrezi jeba poh driver paida kegi?
How much?	karaya tso da?
Please stop here.	mehribani waka delta wadrega
Stop at the next corner.	pa duaima char rahi bandi wadrega
Please hurry.	hala zer-zer lar sha
Please slow down.	mehrabani waka pa karar kooz sha
Please wait here.	mehrabani waka delta intezar waka
I'll get off here.	ze delta kozegum
Where can I hire a taxi?	tixi motor cherta paida kegi?
How much is it for ...?	ter ... poree tso ruppai guary?
one day	yawa wraz
three days	dree wrazee

PASHTO

Useful Words

accident	waqia
air-conditioning	hawa yakhawel
battery	bateree
bicycle	saikel
brake	braik
car	motor
driver's licence	da driver lesens
engine oil	the engine teil
fill up	dakawal
flat tyre	tyre dakawal
headlight	wrandini lightona
highway	loya lar
international driving licence	bainul aquami driving lesens
lorry/truck	loia larai
map	naqsha
motorbike	motor saikel
parking	tamzai
petrol	petrol
radiator	radiator
service station	sarvis steshen
taxi stand	tixi tamzay
three-wheel motorcycle	reksha
tyre	tare

PASHTO

ACCOMMODATION

hotel/inn	otel/sarai
apartment	tamir
dormitory	lailia hastel
guesthouse	mehman khana
youth hostel	da zawanano hastel
campsite	khema

Where is a guesthouse?	mehman khana cherta dai?
I'm looking for a ... hotel.	ghuarum ... otel ta lar shem
cheap	arzan
clean	pak

good	kheh
near-the-city	khar ta negdie
near-the-airport	airport ta negdie
nearby	pe die shawkhwa ke

Booking a Room

There are three kinds of hotels. The highest class hotels have five and four star ratings. These hotels are expensive but a lower price can be negotiated if you are staying for a longer period.

Do you have any rooms/beds available?	kota/besterei sheta?
I'd like a ...	ze ghuarum yawa ...
single room	singel kota
twin room	dua ghebargy koty
quiet room	arama kota
big room	loya kota
bed	bestera
double bed	dua bestery

At the Hotel

How much is it per night?	the yawy shepy tso paisy di?
How much is it per person?	the yawa tan tso paisy di?
Is there a discount for students/children?	the mutal imeno/mashumano depara maraat sheta?
Is hot water available all day?	tola wraz taudy oba sheta?
Can I get a discount if I stay longer?	the ziat wakht osidelo maraat sheta?
Are there any cheaper ones?	koma arzana kota sheta?
Can I see the room first?	lomray kawalai shem kata wogarem?
Could I have a different room?	bela kota newelay shem?
Are there any others?	nory koty sheta?
I like this/that room.	zema dagha/hagha kota khuakha da
It's fine, I'll take this room.	da kha da, ze da kota nisem

PASHTO

I'm going to stay for ...   ghuarum paty shem ...
   one night   yawa shepa
   two nights   dua shepy
   a few days   tso wrazy
   a week   yawa hafta

Can I have the key please?   mata kely raka?
Any messages for me?   mata kum paigham sheta?
Please do not disturb.   taklif me rakawa

Requests & Complaints

It's too ...   da deer ...
   big/small   loi/warookai
   cold/hot   yakh/tode
   dark/dirty   tiara/chatal
   noisy   awaz laroonkai

It smells.   da boi kawi
The toilet is blocked.   tashnab band dai
The door is locked.   darwaza banda jaranda da
My room number is (123).   zema da kamry number (yau selo dirwisht) dai

Please fix it as soon as possible.   da deir zer baraber ka

Checking Out

I'd like to check out now/   ghuarum che otel pridem aus/
   tomorrow.   saba
I'd like to pay the bill.   ghuarum che bill ada kem
Can I leave my luggage here   zema saman delta tso wrazy
   for a few days?   satel kedai shi?
Thank you for your hospitality.   sta de melma paleny na dera shukria

I'm returning ...   ze ragerzem ...
   tomorrow   saba
   in 2-3 days   dua-drey wrazy wrosta
   next week   ratlonky hafta

PASHTO

PASHTO

Useful Words

address	pata	bucket	satal
baggage	saman	door	darwaza
balcony	baranda	key	kely
basin	hauz	light bulb	balb
bathroom/	tashnab (ghusal	lobby	entezar kota
toilet	khana)	lock	jaranda
bed	bestara/kut	luggage	saman
bill	bill	room	kamra
blanket	kampala	shower	shawer

AROUND TOWN

Peshawar is a town straight out of the wild west of the USA. Many streets have boardwalks and outside the Frontier Bank you'll see a guard repleat in bullet belts like Pancho Villa and carrying an enormous shotgun. In Peshawar there are not many women on the streets, and those that are out are veiled. There are many foreign merchants from all over the region trading in the bazaars.

At the Bank

account	hesab
amount	paisey
banknote	lote
buying rate	the akhestelo nerkh
cash	kash
cashier	paisey warkaw oonkai
cheque	chik
credit card	credit card
deposit	amanat
exchange rate	da badlawalo nerkh
exchange	badlawal
foreign currency	kharegy currency
money exchange	paisy badlawal
official rate	doulati nerkh
receipt	raseed
signature	daskhat
travellers' cheque	safari cheque
withdrawal	istel

At the Post Office

I'd like to send ... to (Australia).   ze ghurum che (australia) ta ... walegum

How much does this weigh?   wazen tso mra dai?

address	pata	post code	kode lamber
aerogram	hawaie khat	post office	dok khana
airmail	hawaie dok	registered mail	rejestery khat
envelope	lefafa		
fax	fax	stamps	tiketona
insurance	beema	surface mail	zmakanap post
letter	khat	(urgent)	(arjent ajel)
parcel	parsel	telegram	telegram
postcard	post kat		

Telephone

I want to make a phone call to (Canada).   ghuarum che (canada) ta telepone wakem

What's the number?   tsa lamber dai?

The number is ...   lamber da dai ...

Hello.   hello

Can I speak to ...?   da ... sara khabery kawalai shem?

collect call	kallekt kall
country code	the mulk kode lamber
directory	rahnuma
engaged	magsroof
international call	bainul aqwami kall
(public) telephone	(aam) telepone
telephone number	telepone lamber
wrong number	ghalat lamber

Sightseeing

What's the name of this place?   da die zai noom tsa dai?

Excuse me, what's this/that?   bakhena ghuarum, da hagha tsa shai dai?

PASHTO

Do you have a local map?	da die alaqi naqsha darsara sheta?
Can I take photos here?	mata ijaza sheta che delta potwan wakhlem?
What are the opening hours?	da tsa wakht berta kegy?

How much is the ...?	pe tso dai ...?
admission fee	da dakhely fees
guidebook	rahnama ketab
postcard	post kat

ancient	larghonai	ruins	makhrobat
archaeology	larghone pejandena	sculpture	mujasama jorawal
building	jorawal	sightseeing	manzara lidal
monument	yadgar	souvenirs	yadgar
museum	moziam	statues	mujasemy
old city	pakhwanai khar	theatres	thiater

PASHTO

IN THE COUNTRY

It's best to have a guide and police permission when travelling in villages. Robbers (daku) often plague the rural areas of Pakistan by stopping village buses and robbing passengers.

Weather

What's the weather like today/tomorrow?	nan/saba hawa tsanga da?
The weather's nice today.	nan hawa kha da
Will it rain tomorrow?	saba ba baran washi?
It's hot.	garmi da
It's raining.	baran warigy

It's ...	hawa ... da
fine	dera kha
bright	asman shin
clear/cloudy	rokhana/wrez
dark	tiara

sunny	shin asman
very cold/hot	dera yakhni/garmi
very windy	dera silai
wet	lund

Along the Way

When do we go?	kela ba zu?
Where are we?	mong cherta you?
Can you please tell me how to get to ...?	ta ... ba tsanga warasegum?
How far is it from here to ...?	le dy zaia ter ... pory tsomra lar da?
What will we pass on the way?	pe lara ba kum shayan wagaro?
Are there any things to see here/there?	the lidels war kum shayan sheta?
Let's take a rest here.	delta ba dama waku
Can I have a cup of water/tea?	yawa piala oba/chai sheta?

Seasons

spring	pasarlay	map	naqsha
summer	oray/dobay	mountain	ghar
autumn	manai	mountain	da ghroono
winter	jamai	range	selsala
cave	ghaar	mountain trail	gharanai lar
country	waten (mulk)	mudslide	khawra
desert	sahra		khuaidel
earth	zemeca	river	sind
farm	patai	road	sarak
high plateau	ocheta zemeca	rock	loya tiga
hill	ghunday	season	mosam
hot springs	tod pasarlai	valley	dara
lake	kochnai sind	village	kalai
landslide	zemeca khuaidel	well	kohai

PASHTO

Animals & Birds

buffalo	miekha	monkey	shadi
camel	oukh	mule	qacher
cat	pesho	parrot	toti
chicken	cherga	pig	khaug
cow	ghwa	pigeon	kawtara
crow	kargha	rat	soia
dog	spai	scorpion	larem
donkey	khar	sheep	ged
duck	hilai	snake	mar
eagle	oquab	sparrow	chenchena
falcon	bakha	spider	ankaboot
goat	beza	squirrel	naulai
goose	qaza	tiger	prang
hawk	baz	vulture	tapoos
horse	as	wolf	leva
lion	zmarai		

FOOD

Pashtoons sit on the floor, around a cloth which marks the eating surface. A large serving of pilaf forms the central dish with breads and vegetables to complement. Most often, Pashtoons normally eat with the right hand, but occasionally eat with a spoon.

food stall	khuraka feroshi
market	market
bar	bar
Chinese restaurant	chinaye rasturan
tea house	qahwa khana
restaurant	rasturan
I want to go to a restaurant with Afghani/Chinese food.	ghuaram che the afghani/chinaye khuarakona rasturan ta lar shem

At the Restaurant

Can I see the menu please?	kawalai shem che minu ogorum?
I'll try that.	ze ba da wasakem

I'd like what he's eating.	da hagha khuakha zema khuakhada
Do you have an English menu?	angrezy minu lary?
Can you recommend any dishes?	kum khuarak khe dai?
Do you have a knife and fork?	kashug awe panja lary?
The bill please.	bill rawra
I don't eat meat.	ze ghuakha ne khurem

I would like to have ...	ghuarum che okherum ...
alcoholic drinks	sharab
beverages	mashrubat
green vegetables	sabzi
noodle soup	ashak
pilaf	polave
soup	shorwa
steamed meat pie	manto
stuffed bread	bolani

PASHTO

barfi	sweet meat
da gud da ghuakhy shorwa awe maicha	soup with mutton and noodle flakes
dal aw sabzi	lentils and vegetables
dodai awe kecha ghuakha	buns with mutton
polave awe sabzi	rice pilaf and vegetables
qabilie	rice with dried fruits
samosa	triangular shaped stuffed meat pie
yawa rotai aw kabab	roti bread and kebab

Breakfast, Lunch & Dinner

breakfast	da sahar chai	dinner	da makham dodai
lunch	da gharmy dodai	snack	mukhtasar khuarak

beef	ghata ghuakha	buttermilk	shomlee lassi
bread	dodai	cream	perawai
butter	kouch	eggs	hagay

jam	muraba	orange juice	da malty sharbat
meatballs	arou		
milk	shidy	rice	wrigy
mutton	kecha ghuakha	tea (with milk)	(shudo) chai
noodles	maicha	yoghurt	masta

SHOPPING

Bargaining is welcomed but according to custom, if you shake hands to agree on a price, that price is firm and you should never walk away from the deal without paying.

How many?	tso dany?
How much?	tsomra baia?
I'd like to buy ...	ghuarum che wakhlem ...
I'm just looking.	zema faqat pe kar dai

How much does this cost?	da pe tso dai?
That's very expensive.	da deir gran dai
That's cheap.	da arzan dai
Can you reduce the price?	baia kamawalay shey?

| Where can I buy a ...? | ... cherta akhestelay shem? |

Where's the nearest ...?	kum ... negdy dai?
bazaar	bazar
grocery store	khuraka feroshi
market	market
pharmacy	dawa khana

Sizes & Quantities

a container/ bottle	yau dablai/ botel	50 kilograms	yau man
(half a) dozen	(nim) darjen	100 kilograms	yaua tsata
half/quarter kilogram	nim/yau kilo	one metre	yaw meter
		two kilometres	dua kilometera
five kilograms	yaua darai	three litres	dree litera

PASHTO

Colours

black	toor	orange	naranjy
blue	abi	red	soor
brown	naswary	silver	noqraie
green	shin	white	speen
maroon	gulabi	yellow	zer

HEALTH

It's fairly easy to find specialist doctors who have been trained in England, Australia, the USA or Canada.

I'm sick.	ze naroogh yem
My friend is sick.	zema malgarai naroogh dai
I need a doctor.	ze doktor ta zaroorat larem
I need a doctor who can speak English.	pe angrezi jeba poh dokter ghuarem
I want a doctor that practises western medicine.	da gharbi teb dokter ghuarem
Can you bring a doctor to my room?	kawalai shi zema koty ta dokter rawalay?
Please take me to a doctor.	ma dokter ta warasawa
I've been injured.	ze zakhmi yem
I need an ambulance.	ze ambulance ta zaroorat larem

Can you tell me where the ... is?	cherta dai ...?
clinic	klinik
doctor	dokter
hospital	roghtoon/haspathal
nurse	nars/qabela
pharmacy	dawakhana

I need an English interpreter.	ze english tarjuman ghuarem
I want a female doctor.	kheza doktera pe kar da
Please use a new syringe.	nawai syringe istemal ka
I have my own syringe.	ze khapel syringe larem
I don't want a blood transfusion.	weeny ta zaroorat neshta

PASHTO

PASHTO

I'm not feeling well.	ze kheh ne yem
How long before it will get better?	tsa wakht ba kheh shem?

THE DOCTOR MAY SAY ...

tsa taklif dai?	What's wrong?
cherta zakhmi sho?	Where does it hurt?
tsanga ye?	How are you feeling?
dard sheta?	Do you feel any pain?
teba sheta?	Do you have a temperature?
pakhwa tsa narogha wey?	What illnesses have you had in the past?
cigarete tsekey?	Do you smoke?
sharab tsekey?	Do you drink?
hamal sheta?	Are you pregnant?
da wraze (salore) wakhta (yawa), golai	lit: (4) times a day, take (1) tablet.
da dodai na mekhke/wrosta	before/after meal
da khob na wrandy	before bedtime

Parts of the Body

arm	mata	heart	zera
bone	hadokai	kidney	gurda
ear	ghuag	leg	pandai
eye	stargy	lung	sagai
face	makh	mouth	khula
finger	guty	pulse	rug
foot	pekha	skin	postakai
hand	las	stomach	meda
hair	wikhtan	throat	marai
head	sar	urine	tashi mitiazi

Ailments

I ...	ze ...
have an insect bite	hashary chichalai yem
can't move my ...	khepel ... ne shem khuazawelai
can't sleep	khob ne razi
have a heart condition	zera me khe nadai
lost my appetite	ishteha me ne sheta
have missed my period for ... months.	... miashty najora shawey ne yem
am sore all over	pe tol badan me dard dai
have a high pulse rate	nabz me deir teiz dai
am pregnant	hamela yem
vomited	istefrag (qai) kawem
am weak	kamzarai yem

I have ...	ze ...
altitude sickness	the ghar naroghai
asthma	sa landai
diabetes	diabetes/(da shakar maraz)
diarrhoea	diarrhoea/eshal
dizziness	sargangsi
a fever	taba
hepatitis	parsedel/parsobe
an itch	kharakht/kharash
lice	spega
a migraine	migrin dard
a pain	dard
a stomachache	meda dard
venereal disease	da zena marazona

| I am allergic to antibiotics. | ze de antibiotics sara hasasiat larem |

At the Chemist

May I have ... please?	ghuarum che wakhlem ...
aspirin	aspirin
Band-Aids	palaster

PASHTO

PASHTO

condom
  kandom
cough remedy
  de tookhi dawaie
eyedrops
  da stergo saskai
painkillers
  aram rawronke golai
sanitary napkins
  zanana dusmalona
sleeping pills
  da khob golai
contraceptive pills
  zed hamal golai
travel sickness pills
  da olto zed golai

At the Dentist
dentist
  the ghakho dokter
tooth/teeth
  ghakh/ghakhona
toothache
  ghakh dard
wisdom tooth
  aqal ghakh

Is there a dentist here?
  delta the ghakho
  dokter sheta?
I don't want it extracted.
  ne ghuarum che
  ghakh me wobasy
Please give me an anaesthetic.
  the behoshai dawaie raka
  mehrabani

Useful Words

accident	hadesa
acupuncture	akupankcher
AIDS	AIDZ
antibiotic	antibiotic
antiseptic	antiseptic
blood	weena
blood group/test	da weeny group/maina
contraceptive	the hamal zed dawai
eye drops	da stargy sasky
eye test	da stargo maina
first aid	lomranty
glasses	ainaky
injection	pechkari
menstruation	miashtanai naroghi
optometrist	ainak saz
pneumonia	pneumonia
Red Cross	sra miasht/red kros
specialist	mutakhasis
surgeon	jarah
syringe	pechkary
virus	mikrob
vitamin	vitamin
X-ray	aks/X-ray

PASHTO

TIME, DATES & FESTIVALS
Telling the Time

When?	kala?
What time is it?	tso bajy dhee?

hour	saat	afternoon	da gharmy na wrosta
... o'clock	... bajy		
half past ...	... nimy	noon	gharma
a quarter	paw	evening	makham
morning	sahar	midnight	nima shpa

PASHTO

Days of the Week

Saturday	hafta/shanba	Wednesday	sharow/budh
Sunday	atwar/yakshanba	Thursday	ziarat/jumarat
Monday	peer/doshanba	Friday	juma
Tuesday	naha/mangle		

Months

January	january	July	julaye
February	farwary	August	agust
March	march	September	setember
April	april	October	actober
May	may	November	navember
June	june	December	desamber

The Muslim Calendar

The Islamic calendar is lunar unlike the longer western solar calendar.

muharamul haram	rajabul murajab
safarul muzafar	shuban-ul-mazem
rabi-ul-awal	ramazun-ul-mubarak
rabi-ul-sani	shawal-ul-mukaram
jamadi-ul-awal	ze qaidatul haram
jamadi-ul-akher	ze hejatul haram

Present, Past & Future

today	nan wraz	last week	tera hafta
tonight	nan shpa	tomorrow	saba
(this) week	(da) hafta	next week	ratlonkie hafta
(this) month	(da) miasht	next month	ratlonki miasht
yesterday	paroon		

Festivals & Holidays

Twelfth of rabi-ul-awal — Birth of Prophet Mohammad (P.B.U.H.)

muharram/ashura — Mourning Day particularly for Shiite Muslims commemorating the death of Imam Husain

First of shawal — eid-ul-fitr (marks the end of *ramadan-ul-mubarak* Islamic fast)

Tenth of zil hejja – eid-ul-adha (eid uz-zuha) Three-day Islamic festival commemorating Ibrahim's (Abraham's) attempted sacrifice of his son (Ismail according to Islam) whereby God intervenes providing a sheep for sacrifice instead of the child. It's during this festival that Muslims make their hajj to Mecca. Muslims sacrifice livestock and feast in celebration.

March 23 – Birth of M. Ali Jinah (founder of Pakistan)

August 14 – Pakistan Independence Day

September 6 – Defense Day of Pakistan

November 9 – Birth of Allama Iqbal (national poet of Pakistan)

NUMBERS

0	sefer	30	dirsh
1	yau	39	naha dirsh
2	dua	40	tsalwekht
3	drei	50	panzos
4	tsalare	60	shpeta
5	penza	70	awia
6	shpag	80	atia
7	owa	90	nawi
8	ata	100	sal
9	naha	101	yau sal yau
10	las	110	yau sal las
11	yauolas	115	yau sal penza las
12	dualas	120	yau sal shal
13	diarlas	190	yau sal nawi
14	tsuarlas	200	dua sawa
15	pinzelas	1000	zer
16	shparus	1001	yau zer yau
17	owalas	10,000	las zera
18	atalas	100,000	sal zera
19	nullas	one million	yau million
20	shal	10 million	las milliona
21	yau wisht	100 million	sal milliona
22	dua wisht	one billion	yau billion
23	dir wisht		

PASHTO

PASHTO

EMERGENCIES

Help!	komak!
Danger!	khatar!
Don't move!	harakat me kawa!
Stop.	wadrega
Go away.	lar sha
Listen, we're not interested.	wawra, zamong khuakh ne sho
Call the police.	polees rawoghuara
Call a doctor.	dakter rawoghuara
Could you help me please?	de khudai pe khater zema sa komak waka?
There's been an accident.	waqeda pekha shua
I've been injured.	ze zakhmi shawai yem
I've been raped.	ma takhta yei
I've been robbed.	zemana ghla washwa
Could I please use the telephone?	ejaza da che talipon wakem?
I wish to contact my embassy.	mehrabani waka zema safarat khana khabar ka

Tajik

TAJIK

INTRODUCTION

Tajik is spoken by around five million speakers in seven countries. Of these speakers, just over three million inhabit Tajikistan, one million in Afghanistan and one million live in neighbouring Uzbekistan. Others are spread out in a diaspora reaching Xinjiang, China (36,000), Russia (40,000), and Iran (60,000). There are also significant populations in Kyrgyzstan (35,000) and Kazakhstan (27,000).

Persian, beginning in the 8th century AD, was the lingua franca of the Silk Road from where it spread to China, Iran and Rome. Persian-speaking Muslims spread Islam's influence in Central Asia during that century. Around 1000 AD Persian was unable to resist the powerful influence of the Turkic language from the northeast as the Turkic civilisation gained ascendency. This is not to say that Persian's influence has not been felt in the region. In fact, Persian has had a marked impact on Turkic languages for the past thousand years.

PRONUNCIATION

The Tajik language is written in Cyrillic script in Tajikistan and in a modified Persian-Arabic script in China.

Most Tajik sounds are also found in the English language while a few additional ones must be learned. Intonation is important and this can be learned by listening to Tajiks speak.

Vowels

There are six vowels in the Tajik language and almost all correspond to English sounds, except the sound ö which is produced with rounded lips.

a	as in 'father'
e	as in 'bet'
i	as in 'bill'
o	as in 'go'
ö	as the 'e' in 'her' pronounced with well rounded lips
u	as in 'put'

Tajik Language Area

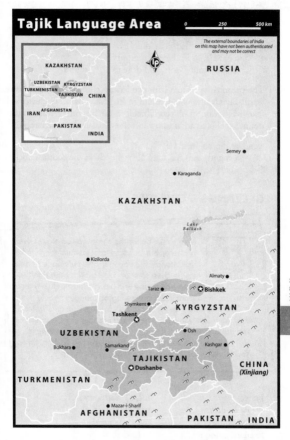

0   250   500 km

The external boundaries of India
on this map have not been authenticated
and may not be correct

KAZAKHSTAN

UZBEKISTAN   KYRGYZSTAN
TURKMENISTAN   TAJIKISTAN   CHINA

IRAN   AFGHANISTAN

PAKISTAN

INDIA

RUSSIA

Semey ●

● Karaganda

KAZAKHSTAN

Lake
Balkash

● Kizilorda

Almaty ●

Taraz ●   ✪ Bishkek

Shymkent ●   KYRGYZSTAN

✿ Tashkent

UZBEKISTAN   ● Osh

Bukhara ●   Samarkand ●   Kashgar ●

TAJIKISTAN   CHINA
(Xinjiang)
✿ Dushanbe

TURKMENISTAN

● Mazar-i-Sharif

AFGHANISTAN   PAKISTAN   INDIA

TAJIK

Consonants

h	with aspiration as in 'haste'
j	as in 'jar'
p	slightly muffled as in 'push'
q	a hard 'k' as in the Arab country 'Qatar'
r	slightly trilled, soft, and close to an 'l' sound

The consonants written with two letters (cluster) are fairly easy to learn. The ch and sh are found in English. The other cluster will take practice but if it's too difficult in the beginning you can pronounce the kh as an 'h' and you will eventually be understood.

ch	as the 'ch' in 'cheek'
kh	a slightly guttural sound like the 'ch' in the Scottish 'loch'
sh	as the 'sh' in 'sheep'

GREETINGS & CIVILITIES

TAJIK

Men shake hands the same way as almost everywhere, but in some cases while they shake right hands, the younger one puts his left hand to the chest to show his respect. Men don't always nod to one another. It's mostly elderly men who do, in response to the greeting of younger people.

Women almost never shake hands while greeting. Instead, they bow slightly to each other and place their right (sometimes left) hand to the heart. If women know each other very well they can hug, and kiss each other on the cheeks two or three times. Young men often hug each other two or three times.

Please.	lutfan (marhamat)
Please sit down.	marhamat shined
Thank you.	rahmat (shukr)
Excuse/Pardon me.	mebakhshed

Never mind.	parvo nadorad/nakuned
Correct.	durust
Good/OK.	khub
That will do.	kifoya ast
Do you understand?	shumo mefahmed?
No.	ne
Yes.	ha
I understand.	man mefahmam
I don't understand.	man namefahmam
Sorry.	mebakhshed
No problem.	hech gap ne
Please wait awhile.	lutfan kame intizor kuned
Where's the toilet?	hojatkhona kujost?

Greetings & Goodbyes

Good morning/day/evening.	assalomu alaykum
	(lit: peace be upon you)
And upon you peace.	valaykum assalom
Good night.	shab bakhayr
How are you?	chi khel shumo?
How is your health?	ahvolaton chi khel?
Where are you going?	kujo rafta istodaed?
What are you doing?	chi kor karda istodaed?
Fine (and you?)	man khub(am va shumo chi khel?)
Not bad.	bad nestam
Goodbye.	khayr
See you tomorrow.	to pagoh
Have a good trip.	rohi safed
See you soon.	to didana
You've been a great help.	shumo kumaki bisyor rasonded

TAJIK

LANGUAGE DIFFICULTIES

I don't speak Tajik/Russian.	man ba zaboni tojik/rus gap mezanad
Do you speak English?	shumo ba zaboni anglisi gap (harf) mezaned?

Do you have an interpreter?	shumo tarjumonro dored?
How do you say that in Tajik?	in chi khel ba zaboni tojik meshavad?
Can you repeat that please?	lutfan takror kuned
Could you speak louder/slower please?	lutfan kame balandtar/ostatar gap zaned
Please point to the phrase in the book.	iltimos, iboraro dar kitob ba man nishon dihed
Just a minute.	yak daqiqa
What does it mean?	ma'noi in chist?

SMALL TALK
Meeting People

Who are you looking for?	ba shumo ki lozim ast?
Is (Akram) home?	(akram) dar khona ast?
Yes, he's here.	ha, vay hamin jost
No, he's not here.	'ne, vay hamin jo nest
What's your name?	nomaton chist?
What's your father's name?	nomi padaraton chist?
Who are you?	shumo kisted?
I'm pleased to meet you.	az shinos shudan bo shumo bisyor khursandam
So am I.	man ham

All gestures in use are those adopted during Soviet time from other Soviet nations. When apologising to someone, you just nod slightly and put your hand to the chest and say mebakhshed. If you want to ask someone about something, you should say mebakhshed at the beginning of your conversation.

What time is it?	so at chand ast?
What's this?	in chist?
Are your parents living?	padaru modaraton zindaand?
My (mother) is alive but my (father) is not.	(modaram) zinda ast vale (padaram) guzashtand
What religion do you believe in?	dini shumo kadom ast?

Nationalities

What country do you come from?	shumo az kadom mamlakat (davlat) omaded?
What ethnic group do you come from?	nazhodi shumo chist?
I come from (the USA).	man az (amriko) omadam

Age

How old are you?	shumo chandsolaed?
How old do you think I am?	ba fikraton man chandsolaam?
I think you are (35) years old.	ba fikram shumo (siyu panj) solaed

Religion

What religion do you believe in?	ba kadam din shumo imon dored?

I'm (a) ...	man ba ... imon doram
Buddhist	budoi
Catholic	katolik
Christian	isavi
Confucian	ta'limoti konfuci
Hindu	hindu
Jewish	yahudi
Muslim	muslim/musulmon

I'm not religious.	man ba din bovari nadoram
Do you attend mosque?	shumo ba masjid meraved?
I attend Mosque every Friday.	man har jum'a ba masjid meravam

Family

This is my ...	in ... ast
father/mother	padari/modari man
husband/wife	shavhari/zani man
son/daughter	pisari/dukhtari man
younger brother	dodari man
younger sister	khohari khurdi man

TAJIK

TAJIK

older brother	akai man
older sister	khohari kalonii man
Are you married?	shumo zandor (m)/shavhardor (f) hasted?
I'm married.	man zandor (m)/shavhardor (f) hastam
I'm single.	man tanho hastam
How many children do you have?	shumo chand farzand dored?
I don't have any children.	man farzand nadoram
How many brothers/sisters do you have?	shumo chand barodar/khohar dored?
I don't have any brothers/sisters.	man barodaru/khohar nadoram

GETTING AROUND

I'd like to go to ... man mekhoham ba ... biravam
How can I get to ...? ba ... man chitavr rafta
metavonam?

Which bus do I take to get bo kadom avtobus man ba
to ...? ... rafta metavonam?
Is there another way to get boz ba onjo chitavr raftan
there? mumkin ast?

What time does the next ... chi vaqt ... oyanda meravad/
leave/arrive? meoyad?
  bus avtobus
  train poezd (qatora)
  plane samolyot (havopaymo)

Where is the ...? kujost ...
  airport aëroport
  bus stop istgohi avtobus
  bus terminal avtovozal (istgohi okhirini
  avtobus)
  train station vokzal
  ticket office dukoni biletfuröshi

Is it far? dur ast?
Yes, it's far. bale, dur ast
It's quite close. bisyor nazdik ast
Can I walk there? piyoda ba onjo rafta metavonam?
How much time will it take ba onjo piyoda raftan chi qadar
to walk there? vaqt darbar megirad?
What's the address? nishona chist?
Please write down the address iltimos, nishonaro ba
for me. man navised
Could you tell the taxi driver iltimos, ba ronandai taksi
the address please? nishonaro fahmoned?
Please draw a map for me. iltimos, ba man kharitaro
kashed

TAJIK

Directions

Tajik people are happy to help travellers and they always give them good directions. They change their voice to a high pitch to indicate long distance, and simply use their hands to indicate directions.

Which direction?	kadom taraf?
Go straight ahead.	mustaqim raved
Turn right/left.	dasti rost/chap garded
direction	taraf
this/that direction	in/on taraf
north/south	shimol/janub
east/west	sharq/gharb
southeast	janubi sharq
northwest	shimoli gharb
uphill/downhill	sari/tagi teppa
left/right	chap/rost
at the corner	dar kunj
up(stairs)/down(stairs)	bolo/poyon
far away	dur
inside/outside	darun/berun
middle	miyon
near	nazdik
near to ...	nazdi ...

Buying Tickets

Where's the ticket office?	kassai biletfuröshi kujost?
I'd like a (1st class) ticket to (Dushanbe).	mekhostam chiptai (darajai avvalro) ba (dushanbe) bikharam
How much is the train to Osh?	chiptai qatora to (osh) chand ast?
Is there a ticket for the bus to (Khokand) today?	shumo chiptai avtobus to (khokand) ba imröz dored?
What is the cheapest fare to (Bishkek)?	arzontarin chipta to (bishkek) chand ast?
There are no tickets.	chipta (bilet) nest

berth number	raqami joy
berth upper/lower	joi boloi/poyoni
cancelled	barham doda shud
confirm	tasdiq kardan
economy class	darajai oddi
1st/2nd class	darajai avval/duyum
one-way ticket	chiptai yaktarafa
return tickets	chiptahoi bozgasht
refund	bargardondani pul
seat	jo
student's ticket	chiptai studenti
ticket office	kassai chiptafuröshi
timetable	jadval

Air

I want to confirm my flight.	mekhoham parvozi khudro tasdiq kunam
This price is higher than normal.	in qimmat az narkhi oddi balandtar ast
aeroplane	samolyot (havopaymo)
airline ticket	chiptai samolyot
customs' (declaration)	(e'lomiyai) gumruk
estimated time of arrival/departure	vaqti tahminii omadan/raftan
gate number	raqami baromadgoh
no smoking	sigaret kashidan man ast
passport	shinosnoma

TAJIK

Bus

Buses are usually crowded in the morning and afternoon, when most people are going to or from work. Buses and trolley-buses don't always run on schedule due to problems with fuel and spare parts.

Is this going to the (bazaar)?	in avtobus tarafi (bozor) meravad?
I want to get off at ...	man mekhoham dar ... bifaroyam

| Please tell me when we've reached that stop. | iltimos, ba man bigued vaqti ki mo ba on istgoh merasem |

| bus | avtobus |
| (long-distance) bus terminal | avtovokzal |

Train

Can you help me find my seat/berth please?	iltimos, ba man yordam kuned dar paydo kardani joi man?
Excuse me, this is my seat.	mebakhshed in joi man ast
Where's the dining car?	vagoni restoran kujost?

dining car	vagoni restoran
express/fast train	qatorai ekspress/tezgard
hard seat (2nd class)	platskart (khujrai umumi)
hard-sleeper (2nd class)	platskart (vagoni khob)
soft-seat (1st sclass)	vagoni narmkursi (darajai avval)
train	qatora

Taxi

To flag down a taxi you should use hand signals. Meters aren't used because of the frequent changes of fares, and inflation. In order to negotiate the fare, you should ask the driver in advance how much the trip is going to cost. Tips aren't usually given.

I'd like to go to ...	mekhostam ba ... biravam
How long does it take to go to ...?	to ... raftan chi qadar vaqt darbar megirad?
Are any English-speaking drivers available?	shumo ronandahoero ki ba zabon anglisi gap mezanand dored?
How much?	chand ast?
Please stop here.	iltimos, injo isted (man kuned)
Stop at the next corner.	dar kunji oyanda isted
Please hurry.	iltimos, teztar
Please slow down.	iltimos, ostatar
Please wait here.	iltimos injo intizor bikashed
I'll get off here.	man injo mefaroyam

TAJIK

Where can I hire a taxi?	dar kujo man taksiro girifta metavonam?
How much is it for one/three day(s)?	baroi yak/se röz chand meshavad?

Useful Words

accident	sadama
air-conditioning	tasfiyai havo
battery	batareya
bicycle	velosiped
brake	tormoz
car	moshin
engine oil	rughani motor
fill up	pur kardan
flat tyre	surohi charkhi moshin
headlight	charoghi pesh
highway	rohi moshingardi tez
(international) driving licence	guvohnomai (bainalkhalqii) ronanda
map	kharita
motorbike	moped
parking	moshinsaroi
petrol	benzin
radiator	radiator
service station	stanciyai khizmatrasonii tekhniki
taxi stand	istgohi taksi
towing a car	kashola karda burdani moshin
tyre	charkh

TAJIK

ACCOMMODATION

Hotels in the cities are mostly state-owned and the rates are fixed. In general, hotels are not comfortable as most of them were built many years ago. In some hotels there are rooms without showers or baths and don't be surprised to find cockroaches or bugs in your room.

hotel/hostel	mehmonkhona	dormitory	khobgoh
apartment	khona	campsite	turbaza

Where is a guesthouse?	mehmonkhona kujost?
I'd like to book a room.	man mekhoham utoqro baroi khud zakhira kunam
I'm looking for a ... hotel.	man mehmonkhonai ... mekobam
cheap	arzon
clean	toza
good	khub
near-the-city	nazdi shahr
near-the-airport	nazdi aeroport
nearby	nazdik

Booking a Room

Do you have any rooms available?	yagon utoqi kholi dored?
Do you have any beds available?	yagon kati khobi kholi dored?
I'd like a ...	mekhostam ...
single room	khonai yak utoqa
twin room	khonai duutoqa
quiet room	utoqi orom
big room	utoqi kalon
bed	kati khob
double bed	kati khobi dukasa

At the Hotel

How much is it per night?	yak shab chand ast?
How much is it per person?	baroi yak nafar chand meshavad?
Is there a discount for students/children?	narkhi makhsusi arzon baroi donishjöyon/ködakon dored?
Can I get a discount if I stay longer?	agar man ziyodtar dar injo istam narkhi utoq baroi man arzontar meshavad yo ne?
Are there any cheaper ones?	arzontar dored?

TAJIK

Can I see the room first?	man metavonam avval utoqro binam?
Are there any others?	digar utoqhoi holi dored?
I like this/that room.	az in/on utoq khösham omad
It's fine, I'll take this room.	bisyor khub, man in utoqro megiram
I'm going to stay for ...	mekhoham ... dar in jo istam
one/two night(s)	yak/du shab
a few days	yakchand röz
a week	yak hafta
Can I have the key please?	iltimos, kalidi utoqro ba man dihed
Is hot water available all day?	obi garm tamomi röz ast?
Could I have a different room?	utoqi digarro ba man doda metavoned?
Any messages for me?	chize baroi man ast?
Please do not disturb.	iltimos, maro muzohimat nakuned

Requests & Complaints

It's too ...	in bisyor ... ast
big/small	kalon/maida
hot/cold	jush/khunuk
dark/dirty	torik/chirkin
noisy	pursado
It smells	in bömekunad
The toilet/sink is blocked	khojatkhona/havz band shudaast
The door is locked.	dar basta ast
My room number is (123).	raqami utoqi man (yaksadu bistu se) ast
Please fix it as soon as possible.	iltimos inro har chi zudtar soz kuned

Checking Out

I'd like to check out	mekhostam holi/pagoh mekhmonkhonaro tark kunam
now/tomorrow	

I'd like to pay the bill.	mekhostam puli ijorai mekhmonkhonaro pardozam
Can I leave my luggage here for a few days?	man metavonam chizhoi khudro dar injo baroi chand röz monam?
Thank you for your hospitality.	rahmat az mehmonnavozii shumo

I'm returning ...	man ... bar megardam
tomorrow	pagoh
in 2-3 days	ba'd az du-se ruoz
next week	haftai oyanda

Useful Words

address	nishona	door	dar
baggage	bagazh	key	kalid
balcony	balkon	light bulb	lamp
basin	havz	lobby	dahlez
bathroom	khojatkhona	lock	qulf
bed	kati khob	luggage	chomadon
bill	hisob	room	utoq
blanket	körpa	shower	dush
bucket	satil	toilet	khojatkhona
caretaker	khizmatgor		

AROUND TOWN

It's possible to stay with local families and if you're going to stay for a short period of time it's usually free. However, if you want to stay longer, you should make arrangements with the hosts. Colour pictures make popular gifts but any gifts are much appreciated.

At the Bank

account	hisob
amount	mablagh (miqdor)
buying rate	qimmati kharid

TAJIK

cash	puli naqd
cashier	kassir
cheque	chek
credit card	varaqai qarz
deposit	depozit
exchange (rate)	(qimmati) tabdil
foreign currency	arzi khoriji
money exchange	tabdili pul
official rate	arzishi rasmi
receipt	khati rasid
signature	imzo
travellers' cheque	cheki roh
withdrawal	pas giriftani pul

At the Post Office

I'd like to send ... to (Australia).	mekhostam ...-ro ba (avstralia) ravon kunam
How much is it?	chand ast?
How much does it weigh?	vazni in chand ast?

address	adres (nishona)
aerogram	aerogramma
airmail	pustai havoi
envelope	lifofa
fax	faks
insurance	sughurta
letter	khat
parcel	amonati pusti
postcard	korti pusti
post code	indeks
post office	pustakhona
registered mail	pustai qayd shuda
stamps	tambrho
surface mail	pustai ma'muli
telegram	telegrom
urgent telegram	telegromi ta'jili

TAJIK

Telephone

I want to make a phone call to (Canada).	mekhoham ba (kanada) telefon kunam
What's the number?	shumorai telefon chist?
The number is ...	shumorai telefoni ... ast
Hello.	allo
Can I speak to ...?	man mekhoham ba ... söhbat kunam

country code	kodi kishvar
directory	rahnamoi telefoni
engaged	masruf ast
international call	zangi bainalkhalqi
public telephone	telefoni umumi
telephone (number)	(raqami) telefon
wrong number	raqami nodurust

Sightseeing

What's the name of this place?	in jo chi nom dorad?
Excuse me, what's this/that?	mebakhshed, in/on chist?
Do you have a local map?	shumo kharitai mahalli dored?
Can I take photos here?	dar injo aqs iriftan umkin ast?
What time does it open/close?	so'ati chand in kushoda boz/ mahkam meshavad?

How much is the ...?	... chand ast?
admission fee	narkhi daromadan
guidebook	rohnamo
postcard	korti pusti

ancient	qadim	ruins	vayronaho
archaeology	bostonshinosi	sculpture	me'mor
building	bino	sightseeing	joi didani
monument	mujassama	souvenirs	armughon
museum	muzey	statues	mujassama
old city	shahri köhna	theatres	teatrho

TAJIK

IN THE COUNTRY

It's better to have your own transport when travelling in the country. There are some bus routes to the nearest villages but buses are not always on time or on schedule.

The countryside is unique and beautiful. The flora is mostly sub-tropical and you can find trees like chinar, archa and oak. There are sanctuaries along the way including Ramit and Tigrovaya Balka. Varzob and Ramit gorges are very close to the capital. Other spots are the Pamir Mountains, the Karategin Valley and Zarafson valley.

Weather

What's the weather like today/ tomorrow?	imröz/pagoh obu havo chi khel ast?
The weather's nice today.	imröz obu havo bisyor khub ast
Will it rain tomorrow?	pagoh boron meborad mi?
It's hot.	garm ast
It's raining.	boron meborad
It's ...	obu havo ...
fine	naghz ast
bright/dark	ravshan/torik ast
clear/cloudy	toza/abrnok ast
very cold/hot	bisyor khunuk/garm ast
very windy	shamoli sakht mevazad
wet	tar ast

Along the Way

When do we go?	kay (chi vaqt) mo meravem?
Where do we meet?	dar kujo mo vo mekhurem?
Where are we?	mo dar kujoem?
Can you please tell me how to get to ...?	iltimos, ba man bigöed chi khel man ba ... rafta metavonam?
What will we pass on the way?	dar roh mo az chi meguzarem?
How far is it from here to ...?	chi qadar dur ast az in jo to ...?
Are there any things to see here/there?	yagon joi didani dar in jo/on jo ast?

TAJIK

Let's take a rest here.	biyoyed dar injo istirohat kunem
Can I have a cup of water/tea?	iltimos, yak piyola ob/choy ba man dihed
I'd like to take a look around your village.	man mekhoham, ki girdu atrofi dehai shumoro tamosho kunam

Seasons

spring	bahor	autumn	tiramoh
summer	tobiston	winter	zimiston
cave	ghor	mountain range	qatorköh
country	kishvar	mountain trail	rohravi kuhi
desert	biyobon	mudslide	selob
earth	zamin	public toilet	khojatkhona
farm	khojagi	river	daryo
high plateau	pahnköh	road	roh
hill	tepa	rock	sanglokh
hot springs	obi garm	seasons	mavsimho
lake	qul	valley	vodi
landslide	selob	village	qishloq
map	kharita	well	naghz
mountain	köh		

Animals & Birds

There aren't many dangerous animals but you should be wary of snakes and poisonous insects such as black widow spiders and scorpions.

bear	khirs	goat	böz
camel	shutur	goose	ghoz
cat	pishak	horse	asp
chicken	chöja	monkey	maymun
crow	zogh	parrot	töti
dog	sag	peacock	tovus
donkey	khar	pigeon	kaftar
duck	murghobi	rat	kallamush
eagle	uqob	sheep	gösfand
fox	röboh	wolf	gurg

TAJIK

FOOD

The table is called dastarkhan and it's either low or directly on the floor. People sit around it, mostly with their legs crossed. The head of the family sits at the centre of the table with guests next to the host. People eat some national dishes, like pilaf, with their right hands, while modern families in the cities prefer spoons and forks. Bread and tea is served first followed by sweets then the main dish.

market	bozor
bar	bar
Chinese restaurant	restorani chini (khitoi)
tea house	choykhona
restaurant	restoran

I want to go to a restaurant with Afghani/Chinese food.	mekhoham ba restorane ki noni afgoni/chini dorad ravam

At the Restaurant

Can I see the menu please?	iltimos, menyuro ba man nishon dihed?
I'll try that.	mekhoham in ta'omro farmoish diham
I'd like what he's eating.	mekhostam ta'ome ki on kas mekhurad farmoish diham
Do you have an English menu?	shumo menyui Anglisiro dored?
Can you recommend any dishes?	yagon ta'omro ba man maslihat karda metavoned?
Do you have a knife and fork?	shumo kordu panja dored?
The bill please.	iltimos, hisobro biyored
I don't eat meat.	man gösht namekhuram
I'd like to have ...	man mekhoham ... farmoish kunam
alcoholic drinks	mashruboti alkogol
beverages	mashrubot
noodles	makaron
pilaf	oshi palov

TAJIK

birinj	rice
kabob	kebab
laghmon	mutton soup with noodle flakes
moshkichiri	lentils and vegetables
oshi palov	rice pilaf and vegetables
sambusa	buns with mutton

Breakfast, Lunch & Dinner

Typical lunches include pilaf, shurbo, mastova or mostoba (rice soup), mantu, and tushbera. Dinner is similar to lunch. Most food is cooked in a traditional metallic bowl called a deg, while non (bread) is baked in the tanur. Dishes differ from region to region, but the central dish is oshi palov or pilaf, which is cooked almost everywhere.

breakfast	noni sahar	lunch	noni nahor
bread	non	milk	shir
dinner	noni shom	tea	choy
eggs	tukhmho	yoghurt	most
foods	khurokvori		

SHOPPING

Travellers should stay away from street merchants and street currency exchange dealers. Bargaining is common and buyers should first offer the lowest reasonable price and then gradually raise it. Handshakes are rarely offered after bargaining.

How many/much?	chand ast?
I'd like to buy ...	man mehostam ...-ro beharam
I'm just looking.	man faqat nigoh karda istodaam
How much does this/that cost?	narkhi in/on chand ast?
That's very expensive.	in bisyor qimmat ast
That's cheap.	in arzon ast
Can you reduce the price?	narkhro arzon karda metavoned?
Where can I buy a ...?	dar kujo man ...-ro kharida metavonam?

TAJIK

Where's the nearest ...?	nazdiktarin ... kujost?
bazaar	bozor
grocery store	magazini khurokvori
market	bozor
pharmacy	dorukhona

Sizes & Quantities

a bottle/container of ...	shishai/quttii ...
dozen	duvozdah
half a dozen	shash
one metre	yak metr
two kilometres	du kilometr
three litres	se litr

Colours

black	siyoh	orange	norinji
blue	nilgun	red	surkh
brown	nasvori	white	safed
green	sabz	yellow	zard

HEALTH

The quality of the doctors is relatively good but the medical treatment depends on your financial situation and the availability of medicine. The majority of doctors are trained in the Tajik Medical University, which ranked very highly among the medical universities of the former Soviet Union. Many doctors trained in Russian universities. All doctors speak Russian but very rarely speak other foreign languages.

TAJIK

I'm sick.	man kasalam
My friend is sick.	rafiqi man kasal ast
I need a doctor.	man dukhtorro kor doram
I need a doctor who can speak English.	man dukhturero, ki zaboni anglisiro medonad, kor doram
I want a doctor that practises western medicine.	dukhturero ki bo tibbi gharbi oshnoi dorad kor doram
Can you bring a doctor to my room?	dukhturro ba injo ovarda metavoned?

THE DOCTOR MAY SAY ...

chi gap ast?	What's wrong?
kujoyaton dard mekunad?	Where does it hurt?
chi khel shumo?/holi shumo chitavr?	How are you feeling?
yagon dardro his mekuned?	Do you feel any pain?
shumo harorat dored?	Do you have a temperature?
chi kasalihoero shumo doshta buded peshtar?	What illnesses have you had in the past?
shumo sigaret mekashed?	Do you smoke?
shumo araq menushed?	Do you drink?
shumo homiladored?	Are you pregnant?
(yak) doru röze (chor) bor iste'mol kuned	Take (1) tablet (4) times a day.
ruze (du bor) ba joi osebdida moled	Apply to the affected area (twice) a day.
pesh az/ba'd az avqot	before/after meal
pesh az ba khob raftan	before bedtime

Please take me to a doctor.	iltimos, maro ba dukhtur bibared
I've been injured.	man majruh shudaam
I need an ambulance.	man yorii ta'jilii tibbiro kor doram
Can you tell me where the ... is?	lutfan ba man bigued ... kujo ast?
clinic	poliklinika
doctor	dukhtur
hospital	kasalkhona (bemorkhona)
nurse	hamshira
pharmacy	dorukhona
I need an English interpreter.	man tarjumoni aglisiro kor doram
I want a female doctor.	man dukhturzanro kor doram

Please use a new syringe.	iltimos, shprici navro istifoda kuned
I have my own syringe.	man shprici khudro doram
I don't want a blood transfusion.	man namekhoham ki khunam zahrolud shavad
I'm not feeling well.	man khudro bad his mekunam

Parts of the Body

arm	dast	kidney	gurda
bone	ustukhon	leg	po (poho)
ear	gush	liver	jigar
eye	chashm	lung	shush
face	ru (ruy)	mouth	dahan
finger	angusht	pulse	nabz
foot	po/poho	skin	jild
hand	dast	stomach	shikam
head	kalla	throat	gulu
heart	dil	urine	peshob

Ailments

I ...   man ...

have an insect bite	maro pashsha gazid
can't move my ...	...-ro junbida nametavonam
can't sleep	khobam nabebarad
have a heart condition	dili man dard mekunad
lost my appetite	man ishtiho nadoram
have a high pulse rate	nabzi man bisyor baland ast
am pregnant	man homiladoram
vomited	man partoftam
am weak	man zaifam

I have ...   man ... doram

asthma	zikki nafas
diabetes	kasalii qand
diarrhoea	darsunravi
dizziness	dardi sar
a fever	tab

TAJIK

hepatitis	zardparvin
an itch	khorishi tamomi a'zoi badan
lice	shabushk
a migraine	dardi sar
pain	dard
a stomachache	dardi shikam

At the Chemist

May I have ... please?	luftan, man ... kor doram?
aspirin	aspirin
cough remedy	dorui surfa
eyedrops	qatrahoi chashm
insect repellent	dorui pashsha
sleeping pills	dorui khob
contraceptive pills	dorui kontroli homiladori

At the Dentist

dentist	dukhturi dandon
tooth/teeth	dandon/dandonho
toothache	dardi dandon

| Is there a dentist here? | man dar injo dukhturi dandonro paydo karda metavonam? |
| I don't want it extracted. | man namekhoham in dandon kanda shavad |

TAJIK

Useful Words

accident	hodisa
acupuncture	suzanzani
AIDS	SPID
antibiotic	antibiotik
antiseptic	antiseptik
blood (group/test)	(gurõhi/sanjishi) khun
eye (drops)	(qatrahoi) chashm
first aid	yorii avval
glasses	aynak
menstruation	qoida
optometrist	dukhturi chashm

Red Cross/Crescent	jam'iyati salibi surkh va hiloli akhmar
specialist	mutak hassis
surgeon	jarroh
syringe	shpric
vitamin	vitamin
X-ray	rentgen

TIME, DATES & FESTIVALS
Telling the time

| When? | kay?/chi vaqt? |
| What time is it? | so'at chand ast? |

hour	so'at
... o'clock	so'at ...
half past ...	nimi ...
a quarter	choryak
morning	sahar
afternoon	ba'd az zuhr
noon	zuhr
evening	shab
midnight	nimishab

Days of the Week

Sunday	yakshanbe	Thursday	panjshanbe
Monday	dushanbe	Friday	jum'a
Tuesday	seshanbe	Saturday	shanbe
Wednesday	chorshanbe		

Months

January	yanvar	July	iyul
February	fevral	August	avgust
March	mart	September	sentyabr
April	aprel	October	oktyabr
May	may	November	noyabr
June	iyun	December	dekabr

TAJIK

The Muslim Calendar

The Islamic calendar is lunar unlike the longer western solar calendar.

muharramul harrom
safarul muzaffar
rabbiul avval
rabbiul soni
jamodiul avval
jamodiul ohir

rajabul murajab
shubonul mozim
ramazonul muborak
shavvolul mukarram
ziqa'datul harrom
zihijatul harrom

Present, Past & Future

| today | imröz | tomorrow | fardo |
| tonight | imshab | yesterday | diröz |

last night	shabi guzashta	this month	mohi jori
(this) week	(in) hafta	last month	mohi guzashta
last week	haftai guzashta	next month	mohi oyanda
next week	haftai oyanda		

Festivals & Holidays

There are two main religious holidays: idi ramazon or id al-fitr and idi qurbon, which are celebrated in all Muslim countries. The Prophet Mohammed's birthday is also celebrated in many places, but not nationally.

March 8
   International Women's Day

March 20-21 navröz
   New Year for Persian-speaking nations (Afghanistan, Iran & Tajikistan)

September 9
   Independence Day

September 20-21 mehrgon
   Tajik Harvest Festival

TAJIK

NUMBERS

0	sifr	30	si
1	yak	39	siyu nöh
2	du	40	chil
3	se	50	panjoh
4	chor/chahor	60	shast
5	panj	70	haftod
6	shash	80	hashtod
7	haft	90	navad
8	hasht	100	sad (yaksed)
9	nöh	101	yaksadu yak
10	dah	110	yaksadu dah
11	yozdah	115	yaksadu
12	dvozdah		ponzdah
13	sezdah	120	yaksadu bist
14	chordah	190	yaksadu navad
15	ponzdah	200	dusad
16	shonzdah	1000	hazor
17	habdah	1001	yak hazoru yak
18	hazhdah	10,000	dah hazor
19	nözdah	100,000	sad hazor
20	bist	one million	yak milyon
21	bistu yak	10 million	dah milyon
22	bistu du	100 million	sad milyon
23	bistu se	one billion	yak milyard

TAJIK

EMERGENCIES

Help!	yordam kuned!
Danger!	khatar!
Don't move!	najumb!
Stop.	isto
Go away.	gum shav
Listen, we're not interested.	gösh kun, mo kor nadorem

Call the police.	miliciyaro jegh zaned
Call a doctor.	dukhturro jegh zan
Could you help me please?	iltimos, yordam kuned?
There's been an accident.	dar injo hodisa surat girift

TAJIK

The Silk Road: Other Languages

THE SILK ROAD:
OTHER LANGUAGES

TASHKORGHANI

The Tashkorghani language (also known as Mountain Tajik) is spoken by the mountain-dwelling Tajik people of Xinjiang and is written in a modified Persian-Arabic script with distinct vowel letters.

In the Pamir mountains, where Tashkorghani is spoken, there are various peoples that are related to the Persian-speaking Sogdians, who were centred in the Samarkand/Bukhara area. The Sogdians were also known as eastern Persians and their civilisation declined around the 8th century. Tashkorghani, however, is so unike Persian that some claim that it isn't Persian at all. So if anything, perhaps they should be called Sogdians.

Pronunciation

Most Tashkorghani sounds are found in the English language, while a few additional ones must be learned. There are eight vowels in the Tashkorghani language and almost all correspond to English sounds except the sounds ö and ü which are produced with rounded lips.

a	as in 'father'
ä	as in 'hat'
e	as in 'bet'
i	as in 'bill'
o	as in 'go'
ö	as the 'e' in 'her' pronounced with rounded lips
u	as in 'put'
ü	as the 'i' in 'bit' with rounded and pushed forward lips
h	as in 'haste'
H	with strong aspiration as in 'Hungary'
j	as in 'jar'
p	slightly muffled as in 'push'
q	a hard 'k' as in the Arab country 'Qatar'

r	slightly trilled, soft, and close to an 'l' sound
ch	as the 'ch' in 'cheek'
gh	similar to the French 'r' (see page 16 for an explanation)
kh	a slightly guttural sound like the 'ch' in the Scottish 'loch'
ng	as the 'ng' in 'rung.'
sh	as the 'sh' in 'sheep.'
th	a very soft 't' sound produced with the tip of the tongue touching the back of the upper teeth
TH	a hard 't' sound pronounced with the tongue curled on the roof of the mouth
ts	as the 'ts' in 'cuts'
zh	as the 's' in 'vision' or 'treasure'

Greetings & Civilities

Please.	marhamat
Please sit down	niTH
Thank you.	rahmat türi
Good/OK.	charj
Do you understand?	wazonddato?
Yes/No.	küdos/nay
Sorry.	afu ka
Where's the toilet?	hajäthono kujur
Good morning/day/evening.	assalamu äläykum
	(lit: peace be upon you)
And upon you peace.	wa'äläykumu salam
Good night.	charj huthm wayn
How are you?	tsarang ta ahwul?
Fine (and you?)	charjam (taw?)
How is your health?	ta tarn durusto?
Have you eaten?	tamoqat khügo?
Goodbye.	khäysh
See you soon.	uza waynan
You've been a great help.	taowat khuch laor yardam chaog

THE SILK ROAD

Language Difficulties

Do you speak English?	tao engiliz ziv lewd chika yo?
I don't speak English/Tajik.	waz engiliz/tujik ziv lewd nachikam
Can you repeat that please?	uz i qatur elev?
Could you speak louder/slower please?	bilandder awuj qati/astoder lev?
Please point to the phrase in the book.	ardi kitub chosam
What does it mean?	di mani tsayz?

Small Talk

What's your name?	ta ato nom tsayz?
What's your father's name?	ta ato-ano nom tsayz?
I'm pleased to meet you.	tü qati balad
So am I.	wazmas bihad khüsh
What country do you come from?	taowat az chidumdowlat yot?
What ethnic group do you come from?	tao tsayz millat?
I come from (the USA).	wazam az (amiriko) yot

This is my ...	yad müyan ...
father/mother	moto/mono
husband/wife	chur/mukhabbät
son/daughter	püts/razen
younger brother/sister	zül würud/yah
older brother/sister	laor würud/yah

Are you married?	tao tay chovgjenj jo?
I'm married.	waz tay chevgjenj
How many children do you have?	tüyan tsund bacho yost?
I don't have any children.	müyan bacho nest
How many brothers/sisters do you have?	tü yan tsund yah/tsund würud yost?
I don't have any brothers/sisters.	müan tsund yah/tsund würud nest

Getting Around

I'd like to go to ...	waz ... setmayj
How can I get to ...?	waz tsayz qati set chikam?
Which (bus) do I take to get to ...?	waz (aftavoz) qati set chikam?
Is there another way to get there?	digar iluj nesto?
What time does it leave/arrive?	chum yothd?
Where's the ...?	... kujur?
bus stop	aftavoz bikät
ticket office	bilat parathod juy
Is it far?	tharo?
Yes, it's far.	ha'a thar
It's quite close.	hüch nizd
How much time will it take to walk there?	piyotho tsun waqter saod?
Please write down the address for me.	wi adiris muri navish
Please draw a map for me.	wi kharito muri tozh
(Which) direction?	(chichidum) yonülüsh?
Go straight ahead.	tüshtar pürud tid
Turn right/left.	tar khayz/chop ghers
north/south	shimal/janub
east/west	sharq/ gharb
left/right	chop/khayz
up/down	tersar/qer
inside	pa darün
outside	wach
near	nizd
I'd like a ticket to (Kashgar).	müri pigan (qashqar) tidichuz
There are no tickets.	ched bilat nist yost
I want to get off at ...	waz ... khofssam
I'd like to go to ...	waz .. setmayj

THE SILK ROAD

How long does it take to go to ...?	... setir tsun wakht tizd?
Are any English speaking drivers available?	engilis ziv wazond shupür yosto?
How much?	tsun pül?

Accommodation

hotel/inn	maymunkhono
apartment	bino
dormitory	yatoq

Where's a guesthouse?	maymunkhono kujuy?
Do you have any rooms/beds available?	khali ched/karabot yosto?
I'd like a single/big room.	muri i ... luzim khalgunj/laor ched
How much is it per night/person?	i Hoban/khalgan tsun pül?
Are there any cheaper ones?	arzunder yosto?
It's fine, I'll thake this room.	iyad ched setir wej, kadi zozam
Can I have the key please?	ochqu muri thoyo?
Could I have a different room?	digar ched tsa zozam saodo?
The room needs to be cleaned.	adi ched i zidor

It's too ...	yad hüch ...
big/small	laor/zül
cold/hot	ish/THüm
dark/dirty	turik/paskano

The door's locked.	diver bawayn sethj
I'd like to check out.	waz khisubut chäygmayj

Around Town

How much is it?	yad tsun pül?
How much does this weigh?	di garuni tsund?
envelope	konwert
letter	khat
post office	poshta
stamps	marka

How do you make a call?	adi telifun tsarang thoyin?
I want to make a phone call to (Canada).	waz (kanada)-ri telifun thom
I want to make an international call to (Australia).	waz (austaliya)-ri kahlagara telifun thom
What's the number?	telifun nümüri tsund?
Hello.	salam

| Do you have a local map? | ta inder kharita yosto? |
| What time does it open? | yam chum at saod? |

In the Country

What's the weather like today/tomorrow?	nür/pigan hawu tsarang?
The weather's nice today.	nür hawu charj at
When do we go?	chum rüwun son?
Let's take a rest here.	od ilo dam zozan
Can I have a cup of water/tea?	i istakam Hats/choy yosto?

| spring | wug | autumn | piz |
| summer | menj | winter | zayn |

Food

Can I see the menu please?	muri tamaq tizimlik wison?
Do you have an English menu?	di ingilischa yosto?
Can you recommend any dishes?	tsarang tamaq yost?
The bill please.	hisubut ka
I don't eat meat.	güHt na horam
I'd like to eat meat/pilaf.	waz güsh/palao horam
I'd like to drink tea/alcohol.	waz choy/haraq bürozam

bar	mäyhuno	lunch	tsuHt
bread	nan	milk	Hevd
breakfast	taryaolitamuq	restaurant	risturon
dinner	Hom	tea	choy
eggs	tühüm	tea house	choyhuno

THE SILK ROAD

süyüqush	mutton soup with noodle flakes
güshnan	nan with meat inside
palao	rice pilaf and vegetables

Shopping

I'd like to buy ...	waz ... zoHt mayj
How much does this/that cost?	palao/yütsun pül?
That is very expensive.	yüqimmat vethj
Can you reduce the price?	wi bawu zül khambon thoyo?
Where can I buy a ...?	waz ... kuju zoHt chikam?
Where's the nearest bazaar/ store?	eng nizdao buzur/dükun kujur?

Health

I'm sick.	waz bemur , mümijuz nist
My friend is sick.	mu dest bemur
I need to see a doctor.	waz akhüdühtürir wesonam
I need a doctor who can speak English.	müri engiliz ziv wazondichuz dühtür luzim
Can you bring a doctor to my room?	müpa yatogh i dühtur vor?
Please take me to a doctor.	amüjiddi (jald) ar dühturhuno yus
I need an ambulance.	müri qütqüzüsh moshina luzim
Can you tell me where the ... is?	müri ... an kujur widi lev tsa?
clinic	dawalash bölüm
doctor	dühtur
hospital	düturhuno
nurse	sestira
pharmacy	dorihuno
I'd like a female doctor	müri i avrat dühtur luzim
It's bleeding	junik naHtizd
How long before it will get better?	chuma soq som?

THE DOCTOR MAY SAY ...

tsayz süt?	What's wrong?
chidum juyik thizd?	Where does it hurt?
tsarangder?	How are you feeling?
thizdiko?	Do you feel any pain?
tuwik soyo?	Are you feverish
pürudat tsayz (tsarang) kasalat sethjit?	What illnesses have you had in the past?
qechinato?	Are you pregnant?
tamoq az pürud/zabu	before/after meal
khuwd chi pürud	before bedtime

Ailments

I ...
   can't sleep
   am weak

waz ...
   Hovdik nachikam
   ujiz

I have ...
   altitude sickness
   dizziness
   hepatitis
   a migraine
   a stomachache

muri ...
   qer kasal
   kol gherd
   qud (jigar) kasal
   kol thizd
   daor dard

At the Chemist

Do you have ...?
   aspirin
   bandages
   condoms

... yosto?
   aspirin
   bent
   biyuntao

Is there a dentist here?

thandun dühtur yosto?

blind	kor	glasses	tsem uynak
dentist	thandun dühtur	teeth	thandun
eye (drops)	tsem (dori)	toothache	thandun dard

Time & Dates

When?	chum?
What time is it?	hozir tsond sut?
hour	suat ...
half past ...	naym suat ...
minute	minot
morning	taryaol
afternoon	payshin
night	Hob

Sunday	yakshanbe	Thursday	payshanbe
Monday	dushanbe	Friday	jüma
Tuesday	seyshanbe	Saturday	shanbe
Wednesday	charshanbe		

today	nür
tonight	biyur
yesterday	Heb
tomorrow (evening)	pigan (biyur)
next week	yetichuz hafto
next month	yetichuz most

Numbers

1	iv	24	vestat tsavur
2	thav	30	si
3	haroy	39	siyat nev
4	tsavur	40	chal
5	pinz	41	chalat i
6	khel	50	pinju
7	üwd	55	pinjuyat pinz
8	voHt	60	atmish
9	nev	70	yatmish
10	thes	80	saksan
15	thesat pinz	90	toqsan
20	vist	100	sad
21	vistat i	101	sadat i
22	vista tha	110	sadat thes

120	sadat vist	1001	i hazur i
190	sadat toqsan	10,000	thes hazur
200	thavsad	100,000	sad hazur
205	thavsadat pinz	one million	i milyun
1000	hazur		

TURKMEN

Turkmen is spoken by 4.5 million people in seven countries. It is principally spoken by the 2.7 million inhabitants of Turkmenistan, a region that is 90% covered by desert. The region lies north of Iran and Afghanistan, and is bordered by the Caspian Sea to the west and Uzbekistan in the east.

The Turkmen language is similar to the western Turkic languages of Azeri and Osman Turkish. Turkmen speakers are also found in the neighbouring countries of Iran (880,000), Afghanistan (580,000), Uzbekistan (130,000), Tajikstan (21,000) and Russia (42,000). There are also nearly 100,000 Turkmen speakers living in Syria.

Pronunciation

The Turkmen language is written in the Cyrillic script in Turkmenistan. The Soviet government imposed the changes from a Persian-Arabic script to a Cyrillic script in the hope of breaking their ties to the Muslim world. After Turkmenistan independence, many countries have pushed the government to change their script. Turkey has pushed for a Roman script and Muslim countries have lobbied for an Arabic script.

a   as in 'father'
ä   as in 'cat'
e   as in 'bet'
i   as in 'bill'
ï   as the 'ye' in 'yes'
o   as in 'go'
ö   as the 'e' in 'her', pronounced with well rounded lips
u   as in 'put'

| ü | as 'i' in 'bit', said with rounded and pushed forward lips |
| y | when between consonants, sounds like the 'e' in 'sister' at the beginning or end of words, as in 'yes' and 'way' |

h	with aspiration as in 'haste'
j	as in 'jar'
p	slightly muffled as in 'push'
q	a hard 'k' as in the Arab country 'Qatar'
r	slightly trilled, soft, and close to an 'l' sound
ch	as the 'ch' in 'cheek'
gh	similar to the French 'r' (see page 16 for an explanation)
kh	a slightly guttural sound like the 'ch' in the Scottish 'loch'
ng	as the 'ng' in 'rung'
sh	as the 'sh' in 'sheep'
zh	as the 's' in 'vision' and 'treasure'

Greetings & Civilities

Please.	bash yustüne
Please sit down.	oturïng
Thank you.	sag bolung
Excuse/Pardon me.	bagïshlang
Good.	yagshï
OK.	bolyar
Do you understand?	siz düshünyasinizmi?
Yes/No.	hawa/yok
I understand.	men düshünyarin
I don't understand.	men düshünemok
Sorry.	bagïshlang
Where's the toilet?	hajathana nirede?
Good morning.	ertiriniz hajïrlï bolsun
Peace be upon you.	essalawmaleykim
And upon you peace.	waleykimessalam
Good night.	gijängiz rahat bolsun
How are you?	siz nähili
How's your health?	sizing saglïgïnïz nähili?
Fine, and you?	onat, a siz?

Have you eaten?	siz ejyam naharlandïnïzmï?
Goodbye.	sag bolung hosh
See you soon.	ene de görüshyanchak
You've been a great help.	siz ulï kömek etdiniz

Language Difficulties

I don't speak English/Turkmen.	men inglische/türkmenche geplamak
Do you speak English?	siz inglische gepleyarsinizmi?
Do you have an interpreter?	sizde terjimechingiz barmï?
How do you say that in Turkmen?	bu sözi türkmenche näme bolyar?
Can you repeat that please?	gaytalasangïzlang?
Could you speak louder/slower please?	siz gatïrak/hayallrak geplesengizläng?
Please point to the phrase in the book.	sözlemi kitapda görkering
What does it mean?	bunung manïsï näme?

Small Talk

What's your name?	sizing adïnïz näme?
What's your father's name?	sizing kakangïzïng adï näme?
I'm pleased to meet you.	siz bilen tanïshmaga shat
So am I.	men hem
What country do you come from?	siz haysï yurtdan?
What ethnic group do you come from?	siz haysï etnik topardan?
I come from (the USA).	men (amerikadan)
This is my ...	be mening ...
father/mother	kakam/ejem
husband/wife	adamïm/ayalïm
girlfriend/boyfriend	gezyän gïzïm/oglanïm
son/daughter	oglum/gïzïm
younger brother	inim
younger sister	gïz jigim
older brother/sister	agam/uyam

Are you married?	siz durmusha chïkanmï? (f)/ siz öylenenmi? (m)
I'm married.	men durmusha chïkan (f)/ men öylenen (m)
I'm not married.	ölenenemok
How many children do you have?	sizing näche chaganïz bar?
I don't have any children.	mening chagam yok
How many brothers/sisters do you have?	sizing näche erker/ayal doganïnïz bar?
I don't have any brothers or sisters.	mening erker/ayal doganïm yok

Getting Around

I'd like to go to ...	men ... gidesim gelyar
How can I get to ...?	... chenli nähili barïp bolar?
Which (bus) do I take to get to ...?	men haysï (avtobusa) ... chenli münmeli?
Is there another way to get there?	ol ere bashga yel barmï?
What time does it leave/arrive?	hachan indikli .. ugrayar/gelyär?
Where's the ...?	... nirede?
bus stop	avtobusa bikät
bus terminal	avtovokzal
ticket office	kassa
Is it far?	ol dashmï?
Yes, it's far.	hava, ol dash
It's quite close.	bu gatï yakïn
Can I walk there?	piyada gitsem bolarmï?
How much time will it take to walk there?	piyada gitsem näche wagt gerek bolar?
What's the address?	adres näme?
Please write down the address for me.	adresi mening üchin yazsangïzlang
Could you tell the taxi driver the address please?	taksi sürüja adresi aysanïzla?

Please draw a map for me.	mening üchin karta cheksenizle
Which direction?	haysï ugurda?
Go straight ahead.	göni yone giding
Turn right/left.	saga/chepe al
north/south	demirgazïk/günorta
east/west	gündogar/günbatar
left/right	chep/sag
up/down	yokarï/ashak
inside/outside	ichine/dasharï
near	yakïn
I'd like a ticket to (Ashgabad).	mana (ashgabat) üchin bilet gerek
There are no tickets.	bilet yok
Is this going to the (bazaar)?	bu (bazara) gidyärmi?
I want to get off at ...	men ... düshesim gelyar
Please tell me when we've reached that stop.	shol duralga (ostanovka) baramïzda mana aytsanïzlang
I'd like to go to ...	men ... gitmekchi (gitjek)
How long does it take to go to ...?	... barmak üchin näche wagt gerek?
Are any English speaking drivers available?	inglische gepleyan sürijiler barmï?
How much?	näche?

Accommodation

hotel	mïhmanhana
inn	kervensaray
dormitory	umumï yashayïsh jayï
youth hostel	yashlarïng umumï yashayïsh jay
Where's a guesthouse?	mïhmanlar üchin jai nirede?
I'd like to book a room.	men otag (nomer) zakaz etjek
Do you have any rooms available?	sizde bosh otag barmï?
Do you have any beds (places to sleep) available?	sizde bosh krovat (yatmaga yer) barmï?

I'd like a ...	manga ... gerek
single room	bir adamlïk otag
quiet room	yuwash otag
big room	ulï otag

How much is it per night?	bir gija näche?
How much is it per person?	bir adam üchin näche?
Are there any cheaper ones?	arzanrak otaglar barmï?
I like this/that room	men bu/ol otagï halayan
Can I have the key please?	acharï bersenisle?
Could I have a different room?	mana bashga otag bersenisle?
Please do not disturb.	azar bermangle, päsgel bermäng

It's too ...	bu yoran ...
big/small	ulï/kichijik
cold/hot	sowuk/gïzgïn (ïssï)
dark/dirty	garangkï/hapa
noisy	galmagalï (showhunlï)

The door's locked.	gapï gulplï
I'd like to check out.	men gidip baryan
Can I leave my luggage here for a few days?	birki günlük zatlarïmïzï galdïrsak bolyarmï?
I'm returning tomorrow	men ertir gaydïp gelyän
Thank you for your hospitality.	sizing mïhmansöyüjiligingiz üchin minnet dar

Around Town

I'd like to send ... to (Australia).	men (avstraliya) ... ibermekchi
How much is it?	näche?
How much does this weigh?	munïng agramï näche?

address	adres	post office	pochta
airmail	aviyapochta	postcard	otkrïtka
envelope	konvert	stamps	markalar
letter	hat	telegram	telegram
parcel	posilka	telex	teleks

I want to make a phone call to (Canada)	men (kanada) telefon jang etmekchi
What's the number?	nomeri näme?
The number is ...	nomeri ...
Hello.	allo, salam

What's the name of this place?	bu yering adï näme?
Do you have a local map?	sizde yerli karta barmï?
What time does it open/close?	bu hachan achyar/yapyar?

In the Country

What's the weather like today/ tomorrow?	shu gün/ertir howa nähili (bolar)?
The weather's nice today.	shu gün howa gowï
Will it rain tomorrow?	ertir yagmïr yagarmï
Where are we?	biz nirede?

Can you please tell me how to get to ...?	... nähili barsam bolyar?
How far is it from here to ...?	shu yerden ... chenli nähilräk dash?
Can I have a cup of water/tea?	mana bir käse suw/chay ichip bolarmi?

Food

Can I see the menu please?	menyu barmï?
I'll try that.	men onï dadïp göreyin
I'd like what he's eating.	shol adamïng iyyän zadïndan manga-da bering
Do you have an English menu?	sizde inlis menu barmï?
Can you recommend any dishes?	haysï naharï hödürlarsingiz?
I don't eat meat.	men et iyemok
The bill please.	hasap kagïzï bering
I'd like to have ...	men ... alasym geljar

güshnan	nan with meat inside
bulka bilen goyun eti	buns with mutton
ashlï goyun chorbasï	mutton soup with noodles
palaw we gök yonyumleri	rice pilaf and vegetables
non bilen kebap	nan bread and kebab
meryimek bilen gök yonyumleri	lentils and vegetables
palaw	pilaf

bread	chörek
breakfast	ertirlik nahar
dinner	agshamlïk nahar
eggs	yumurtga
food stall	kiosk
lunch	günortanlïk (gushlik) nahar
market	bazar
milk	süyt
restaurant	naharhana/restoran
Russian restaurant	rus restorany
snack	eniljek nahar
tea	chay
yoghurt	gatïk

Shopping

How many?	näche sanï?
How much?	näche?
I'd like to buy ...	men ... aljak
How much does this cost?	bu näche?
That's very expensive.	ol gatï gïmmat
That's cheap.	ol arzan
Where can I buy a ...?	men ... nirede alsom bolyar?
Where is the nearest bazaar/ grocery store?	ing golaj (bazar)/(iymit magazini) nirede?

a bottle/container of	bir chüyshe/ gap
dozen	on iki sanï
half a dozen	altï sanï
one metre/kilometre/litre	bir metr/kiilometr/litr

Health

I'm sick.	men sïrkav
My friend is sick	mening dostum sïrkav
I need a doctor (who can speak English).	manga (inlische bilyän) doktor gerek
Can you bring a doctor to my room?	otagïma doktor chagïrïp bilyängizmi?
Please take me to a doctor.	meni doktora äkiding

Can you tell me where the ... is?	... nirededigini aydïp bilyängizmi?
clinic	poliklinika
doctor	doktor
hospital	keselhana/gospitals
nurse	shepagat uyasï
pharmacy	dermanhana

I need an English interpreter.	mana inlis dilinden terjimechi gerek
Please use a new syringe.	täze shprits ullansanïzlang

I have my own syringe.	mende öz shpritsim bar
I don't want a blood transfusion.	men gan goybermani islämok
I'm not feeling well.	saglïgïm gowï däl
How long before it will get better?	hachan gowulasharïn

THE DOCTOR MAY SAY ...

näme boldï?	What's wrong?
sizing niräniz agïryar?	Where does it hurt?
siz özinizi nähili duyyarsïnïz?	How are you feeling?
agïryarmi?	Do you feel any pain?
siz sonkï wagtda nähili kesel bilen kesellapdiniz?	What illness have you had in the past?
siz göwrelimi?	Are you pregnant?
hersinden (bir) tabletka günde (dört) gezek iching	Take (1) tablet each (4) times a day.
degishli yere günde (iki) gezek chalmalï	Apply to the affected area (twice) a day.
nahardan öng	before meal
nahardan song	after meal
yatmankang	before bedtime

Ailments

I ...	men ...
can't move my ...	öz ... gïmïldadïp bilemok
can't sleep	yatïp bilemak
have missed my period for ... months.	bilim ... ay bäri achïlanak
am pregnant	göwreli
am weak	güyjüm yok

I have ...	mende ... bar
altitude sickness	dag keselim
asthma	astma
diabetes	diabet kesel
hepatitis	gepatit

At the Chemist

Do you have ...?	men ... dĭïp bilerinmi?
aspirin	aspirin
bandages	bint
condoms	perservativ
painkillers	agĭrĭnĭ ayïryan derman
sanitary napkins	gigienik paket
sleeping pills	uklamak üchin derman
contraceptive pills	göwreli boldurmayan derman
travel sickness pill	yürek bulashmadan derman

At the Dentist

dentist	dish doktorï
teeth	dishler
toothache	dis agĭrsï
Is there a dentist here?	bu yerde dish doktorï barmi?
I don't want it extracted.	dishimi sogurmalï däl
Please give me an anaesthetic.	anasteziya dermandan manga bering

Time & Dates

When?	hachan?
What time is it?	sagat näche?
hour	sagat
... o'clock	sagat ...
half past ...	... ing yarï
a quarter (15 minutes)	chäryek sagat (on bäsh minut)
morning	ir
afternoon	gündiz
evening	agsham

Sunday	ekshenbe	Thursday	penshenbe
Monday	düshenbe	Friday	anna güni
Tuesday	sishenbe	Saturday	shenbe
Wednesday	charshenbe		

THE SILK ROAD

today	shu gün	(this) month	(shu) ay
tonight	shu gün agsham	tomorrow	ertir
(this) week	(bu) hepde	next week	indiki hepde

January	yanvar	July	iyul
February	fevral	August	avgust
March	mart	September	sentyabr
April	aprel	October	oktyabr
May	may	November	n'oyabr
June	iyun	December	dekabr

Numbers

0	nul	50	elli
1	bir	60	altmïsh
2	iki	70	yetmish
3	üch	80	segsen
4	dört	90	togsan
5	bäsh	100	yüz
6	altï	101	yüz bir
7	yedï	110	yüz on
8	sekiz	115	yüz on bäsh
9	dokuz	120	yüz yigrimi
10	on	190	yüz togsan
11	on bir	200	iki yuz
15	on bäsh	1000	bir müng
20	yigrimi	1001	bir müng bir
21	yigrimi bir	10,000	on müng
30	otuz	100,000	yüz müng
40	kïrk	one million	bir million

Emergencies

Help!	kömege!
Danger!	howplï!
Stop.	dur
Call the police.	politsiyanï chagïrïng
Call a doctor.	doktorï chagïrïng

Could you help me please?	kömek bersengizläng?
There has been an accident.	avariya bolupdïp
I've been raped.	meni zorladïlar
I've been robbed.	meni ogurladïlar
Could I please use the telephone?	jang etsem bolyarmï?

BURUSHASHKI

Burushashki is spoken in central Hunza, upper Nagar, Yasin, Ishkoman and northern Chitral. Its origins are obscure, but it's quite ancient. Its difficult structure makes it nearly impossible for outsiders to master; there are said to be 38 plural forms, and words change form at both ends depending on context.

Essentials

Hello.	leh
Goodbye.	khuda hafiz
How are you?	behal bila?
I'm fine.	je shuwa ba
Thank you.	bakhshish
Yes./No.	awa/beya
Maybe.	meimi
Pardon/Forgive me.	maf eti
What's your name?	behsan guik bila?
My name is (John).	ja aik (jan) bila
Where are you from?	oom amilim ba?
How old are you?	behsen umur bila?
I'm (20) years old.	ja (altar) den bila
Do you speak English?	angrezi juchi bila?
How much does this cost?	behsan koi mad bila?
Where is ...?	... amili bila?
I'm lost.	awalaam
Go away!	ni!

Useful Words

north/south	kanjoot/jenoos	beautiful	khushroi
east/west	jilmanas/	delicious	mazadar
	burmanas	left/right	ghaipa/doipa
very	ghafeh	this/that	yem/ya
good/bad	baaf/shaak	here/there	koleh/eleh

Family

man/woman	hir/gus
my father/mother	au/ami
your father/mother	gu/gumi
my son/daughter	ei/ai
your son/daughter	gui/goi
my brother/sister	acho/ayas
your brother/sister	gochu/guyas
husband/wife	a'uyar/a'us
friend	shugulo (m)/shuguli (f)

Accommodation

single/double room	hin/altan siseh kamara
key	chei
room	kamera
toilet	chukaang

Food

I'm vegetarian.	ja siruf hoi shehchaba
Do you have (tea)?	(chai) bila?
food	shias
dry cheese	kurut
egg	tigan
food/bread	shapik
meat	chaap
noodle soup	daudo
rice	briw/bras
white cheese	burus
whole-wheat bread	phitti
vegetable	hoi

yoghurt	dumanu mamu
tea	chai
green tea	sabaz chai
(drinking) water	(minas) tsil

Time

what time is it?	behsan kandila?
It's (10) o'clock.	mu (torimi) gharibi
when?	behshal?
today	khultu
tomorrow	jimeleh
yesterday	sabur

Numbers

1	han	20	altar
2	alto	30	altar torumo
3	usko	40	alto altar
4	walto	50	alto altar torumo
5	tsundo	60	iski altar
6	mishindo	70	iski altar torumo
7	talo	80	walti altar
8	altambo	90	walto altar torumo
9	huncho	100	ta
10	torumo	1000	saas

KHOWAR

Khowar (Chitrali) is the speech not only of Chitral proper but of Ishkoman, Yasin and Ghizar on the Gilgit side of the Shandur Pass.

Essentials

How are you?	tu keecha asoos?
Very well, thanks.	bojam, shukria
Please.	mehrbanni khori
Yes./No.	dee/no
Where is (Drosh)?	(drosh) kura sher?
A little.	kam

THE SILK ROAD

Useful Words

bed	jen
mountain	zoom
(very) good/bad	(bo) jam/shum
beautiful	choost
high	rang
father/mother	taat/naan
brother/sister	brar/ispisar
husband/wife	mosh/bok
bread	shapik
meat	pushoor
water	oogh
today	hanoon
yesterday	dosh
tomorrow	choochi

Numbers

1	yi	7	sot
2	ju	8	osht
3	droi	9	niu
4	chor	10	jiush
5	ponj	20	bishir
6	choi	100	shor

KOHISTANI

Kohistani is spoken in northern Swat and Indus Kohistan. It's a mish-mash of Shina, Pashto, Urdu, Persian and other languages, and varies from one village to the next.

Essentials

Hello.	asalaam aleikum
Goodbye.	hudar hawala
Good.	suga/mihta
Thank you.	shukria
Yes./No.	ah/ni

Useful Words

high valley/pass	dara
mountain	kor
name	na
good/bad	mishto/khacho
happy	khush
expensive	keimeti
hot/cold	tato/shidalo
left/right	kabu/dachinu
this/that	anu/ro
here/there	adayn/al

Family

man/woman	maash/garyu
father/mother	aba/ya
son/daughter	puch/dhi
brother/sister	zha/bhyun
(my) friend	(mil) doost

Food

bread	gwel	tea	chai
egg	ana	vegetable	sabzi
meat	masu	water	vi/wi
milk	chir	yoghurt	dudi

Time

today	aaz	now	uskeh
tomorrow	okot	(two) o'clock	(du) masma

Numbers

1	ek	8	aat
2	du	9	naan/nau
3	cha	10	daash
4	sawur	20	bish
5	paz	100	shol
6	sho	1000	zir
7	saat		

MANDARIN

 Mandarin (or Putonghua, 'common language') is China's official language, the dialect of Beijing and the speech of bureaucrats. Basic spoken Mandarin is surprisingly easy: no conjugation of verbs, no declensions and word order like English. The hard parts are pronunciation and tones.

Pronunciation

Mainland China's official Romanised 'alphabet' of Chinese sounds is called Pinyin. It's very streamlined, but the sounds aren't always self-evident. Some letters that don't sound quite like English are as follows:

Consonants: q ('ch'); x ('sh'); zh ('j'); z ('dz'); c ('ts'); r (tongue rolled back, almost 'z').

Vowels: a ('ah'); er ('ar', American pronunciation); ui ('oi' or 'wei'); iu ('yoh'); ao ('ow' as in 'now'); ou ('ow' as in 'low'); e ('uh' after consonants); ian ('yen'); ong ('oong'); u ('oo', or sometimes like 'ü': say 'ee' with your mouth rounded as if to say 'oo').

A given sound has many meanings depending on its tone. But sometimes you can get away without tones because the Chinese try hard to figure out what you mean. Syllables aren't stressed strongly.

Essentials

Hello. (lit: are you well?)	ni hao
Goodbye.	zaijian
Thank you.	xiexie
Please.	qing
Excuse me.	dui bu qi
Yes.	dui
No.	bu dui/shi
Where's (the toilet)?	(cesuo) zai nar?
Do you have (hot water)?	(kai shui), you mei you?
How much does it cost?	duo-shao qian?
Too expensive!	tai gui-le!

Enough!	gou le!
Where are you going?	qu na li? or qu nar?
Is it allowed?	ke bu keyi?
Can you speak English?	ni hui shuo yingyü ma?
I can't speak Mandarin.	wo bu hui shuo putonghua
Do you understand?	ni dong ma?
I don't understand.	wo ting bu dong

Useful Words

beautiful	hao-kan
broken	huai-le
buy/sell	mai
expensive/cheap	gui/pianyi
go	qu
good/bad	hao/huai
happy	gaoxing
here/there	zhe-li/ner
left/right	zuo/you
like	xihuan
live/reside	shenghuo
map	ditu
money	qian
open (for travel)	kaifang
toilet paper	weisheng zhi

Family

father/mother	baba/mama
husband/wife	zhangfu/qizi
son/daughter	erzi/nuer
friend	pengyou

Getting Around

airport	feiji chang
bicycle	zixingche
bus (station)	qiche (zhan)
ticket to (Kashgar)	dao (kashgar) de piao
train station	huoche zhan

THE SILK ROAD

Accommodation

double/single room	shuang-ren/dan-ren fangjian
guesthouse/hotel (cheaper)	binguan/lüguan
key	yaoshi
shower	linyu
telephone	dianhua
toilet	cesuo

Around Town

airmail	hang-kong
bank	yinhang
hospital	yiyuan
post office	you-ju
Public Security Bureau	gong-an ju
stamp	you-piao

Food

beef	niu rou
beer	pijiu
bill/check	maidan
boiling water (for tea)	kai shui
bread	mianbao
chicken	ji rou
chopsticks	kuaizi
egg	jidan
fried noodles	chaomian
green vegetable	qingcai
hot chillies	lajiao
menu	caidan
milk	niu nai
MSG	wei-jin
mutton	yang rou
restaurant	fanguar
rice	fan
steamed/fried rice	mifan/chaofan
tea	cha

Time

when (date/time)?	ji hao/dian?	now	xianzai
today	jintian	(five) o'clock	(wu)-dian
tomorrow	mingtian	half-past (eight)	(ba)-dian
yesterday	zuotian		ban

Numbers

1	yi	9	jiu
2	er (number 2)	10	shi
	liang (counting)	11	shi yi
3	san	20	er shi
4	si	21	er shi yi
5	wu	30	san shi
6	liu	100	yi bai
7	qi	200	liang bai
8	ba	1000	yi qian

MONGOLIAN

Mongolian is a member of the Ural-Altaic family of languages which includes Finnish, the Turkic languages and Korean. Mongolian is a difficult language for English-speakers to learn, in part because the words are very long and pronunciation differs radically from Indo-European languages.

Essentials

Hello.	sain bainuu
Goodbye.	bayartai
Thank you.	bayarlaa
I'm sorry.	uuchlaarai
I don't understand.	bi oilgokhgüi bain
I understand.	bi oilgoj bain
Do you speak English?	ta angilar yair daguu?
Yes/No.	tiim/ügüi

Useful Words & Phrases

Where's the toilet?	jorlong khaan baidag ve?
How much does it cost?	en yamar üntei ve?
That's very expensive!	yaasan üntei yum be!
post office	shuudan giin salbar
stamps	shuudangiin mark
postcard	il zakhidal
telephone	utas/telefon
north/south	khoid/urd
east/west	züün/baruun

Getting Around

I'm lost.	bi toorchihloo
Where is the ...?	... khaan bain ve?
map	gazryn zurag
train station	galt tergenii buudal
bus station	avtobusny buudal
to the right/left	baruun/züün tiish
straight ahead	chigeree

Accommodation

hotel	zochid buudal
room	öröö
single/double room	neg/khoyor khünii öröö
cheap room	khyamd öröö

Time

What time is it?	kheden tsag hed bolj bain?
... o'clock	... tsag bolj bain
yesterday	öchigdör
today	önöödör
tomorrow	margaash

Monday	davaa	Friday	baasang
Tuesday	myagmar	Saturday	byamb
Wednesday	lkhavag	Sunday	nyam
Thursday	pürev		

Numbers

1	neg	10	arav
2	khoyor	11	arvan neg
3	gurav	12	arvan khoyor
4	döröv	13	arvan gurav
5	tav	20	khori
6	zurgaa	31	guchin neg
7	doloo	100	zuu
8	naim	101	neg zuun neg
9	yös	1000	myang

Emergencies

Help!	tuslaarai!
Thief!	hulgaich!
Fire!	gal!
Call the police.	tsagdaa duudaarai
I'm sick.	bi övchtei bain
Please take me to the hospital.	namaig emnelegt khürgej ognüü

RUSSIAN

Russian grammar may be daunting, but your travels will be far more interesting if you can say a few words. Two common words that you are sure to use are zdrastvooytyeh, the universal 'hello' and pazhahloohstuh, the multi-purpose word for 'please', 'you're welcome' and more.

Essentials

Hello.	zdrastvooytyeh
Good morning.	dohbrayuh ootra
Good afternoon/evening.	dohbri dyen/vyehchir
Goodbye.	dasfidanya[
How are you?	kak dyilah?
Yes/No.	da/nyet
Thank you (very much).	spuhseeba (balshoyuh)
Pardon me.	prasteetyeh, pazhahloohstuh
No problem/Never mind.	nichevoh (lit: nothing)
Good/OK.	kharashoh
bad	plohkha
this/that	ehta/toh
I don't speak Russian.	ya nye gavaryu paruski
I don't understand.	ya nye pahnimahyu
Do you speak English?	vih gavareetyeh paangleeski?
Will you write it down, please?	zuhpisheetyeh, pazhahloohstuh?
Can you help me?	pamageetyeh mnyeh, pazhahloohstuh?
May I take a photo?	fatagruhfeeravut mozhna?
I need ...	mnyeh noozhna ...
Where is ...?	gdyeh ...?
toilet	tualyet
translator	pirivohtchik

Getting Around

When does it leave?	kugda ahtlitayit?
ticket/s	beelyet/i
baggage	buhgahzh
arrival	pribihtiyeh

departure	ahtpruvlyeniyeh
airport	ahehraport
check-in	rigistrahtsiuh
customs	tuhmohzhnyah
bus	uftohboos
bus stop	ahstanovkuh
railway station	zhilyeznuh darohzhni vahgzahl
train	poyest
seat/place	myesta
taxi	tahksee

Accommodation

How much is a room?	skolka stoeet nohmyer?
hotel	gusteenitsuh
room	nohmyer
boiled water	keepyuhtok
too hot/stuffy	zharka/dooshna

Around Town

I'm lost.	ya zuhbludeelsuh (m)/ zuhbludeelus (f)
How much is it?	skolka stoeet?
street	ooleetsuh
building	korpoos
museum	muzyey
north/south	syehvir/yook
east/west	vastok/zahpuht
to/on the left	nuhlyehva
to/on the right	nuhprahva
straight ahead	pryahma
here/there	toot/tahm
money	dyengi
currency exchange	ahbmyehn vahlyutuh
bank	bahnk
travellers cheques	darohzhnihyeh chehki
post office	pohchtah
stamp	markuh

telephone	tilifohn
shop	muhguhzyin
market	rihnuk
pharmacy	uptyeka
souvenirs	suvineeri
open/closed	ahtkrit/zuhkrit

Food

breakfast	zahftruk
lunch (afternoon meal)	abyet
dinner	oozhin
restaurant	ristarahn

Time

What time is it?	katori chahs
At what time?	fkatorum chuhsoo?

Monday	panidelnik	Friday	pyatnitsuh
Tuesday	ftornik	Saturday	subohtuh
Wednesday	srida	Sunday	vaskrisenyuh
Thursday	chitverk		

Numbers

0	nohl	30	treetsut
1	ahdyin	40	soruk
2	dva	50	pidisyaht
3	tree	60	shizdisyaht
4	chitiryeh	70	syemdisyit
5	pyaht	80	vosimdisyit
6	shest	90	divyinohsta
7	syem	100	stoh
8	vosyim	500	pyuhtsoht
9	dyevyut	1000	tihsuhchuh
10	dyesyut	2000	dvyeh tihsuhchi
11	ahdyinutsut	10,000	dyesyut tihsuhch
20	dvahtsut	100,000	stoh tihsuhch
21	dvahtsut ahdyin	1 million	ahdyin miliohn

Emergencies

I'm sick.	ya bohlyin (m)/bahlna (f)
I need a doctor.	mnyeh nuzhin vrahch
hospital	bohlnitsuh
police	mileetsiyuh
Fire!	pazhar!
Help!	na pohmushch!/pamageetyeh!
Thief!	vor!

SHINA

Shina is spoken in lower Hunza and Nagar, Gilgit and its valleys, Chilas and north-east Indus Kohistan. Meanings are often expressed by tones, so only the simplest words are given here.

Essentials

Hello.	ala
Goodbye.	huda hafiz
How are you?	je kal han?
Fine.	mishto han, mehrbani
Please.	mehrbani teh
Thank you.	bakhshish
Yes/No.	awa/neh
Maybe.	bebey
What's your name?	tei jek nom han?
My name is (John).	mei nom (jan) han
Where are you from?	tu konyo hano?
I'm from	ma ... hanoos
Do you speak English?	toot angrezi wa nah?
I don't understand.	ma (neh) parudus
How much is it?	jek garch han?
Where is ...?	... kon han?
I like (Gilgit).	mas (gilgit) pasantamus
I'm vegetarian.	mas siruf shakamus

Useful Words

hot spring	tato uts
house	goht
mountain	chish
river	sin
single/double room	ek mushai/du musho kamara
valley	gah
left/right	kabo/dachinu
north/south	shimal/jinu
east/west	jilboik/burboik

Family

man/woman	manuzho/chei
father/mother	malo/ma
husband/wife	musha/jama
son/daughter	pooch/di
brother/sister	zha/sa
friend	somo

Food

food	koig	wholewheat bread	chupatti/dudurtik
apricot	jeroti	vegetable	sha
egg	haneh	yoghurt	mutu dut
food/bread	tiki	milk	dut
meat	moz	tea	chai
rice	briw	water	wei
salt	paju		

Time

What time is it?	je ken han?
It's (10) o'clock.	(dai) bashegen
When?	gareh?
today	aach
tomorrow	lushteh
yesterday	bala
now	ten

Monday	tsandura	Friday	shukura
Tuesday	angaro	Saturday	shimsher
Wednesday	bodo	Sunday	adit
Thursday	berespat		

Numbers

1	ek	20	bi
2	du	30	bigadai
3	cheh	40	dubyo
4	char	50	dubiga dai
5	poe	60	shabyo
6	sha	70	shabyoga dai
7	saat	80	charbyo
8	aash	90	charbyoga dai
9	nau	100	shal
10	dai	1000	saas

WAKHI

Wakhi is the speech of the Wakhi tribe of Tajik people in Gojal and Afghanistan's Wakhan Corridor. It's very similar to the speech of other Tajiks in the Tashkurgan region and Tajikistan.

Essentials

Hello.	asalaam aleikum
Goodbye.	khudar hafiz
How are you?	chiz hawli?/baaf ateya?
I'm fine.	uzum baaf
Yes/No.	yau/neis
I don't know.	dishma
Please.	mehrboni
Thank you.	shobosh
Excuse me/Sorry.	mofsar
What's your name?	ti noongi chiz?

My name is (John).	zhu noongi (jan)
Where are you from?	tut koom dyoren?
I'm from ...	uzum ...
Do you speak English?	torezh angrezi vizta?
I (don't) understand.	mazhe malum tei (nahst)
Where is ...?	... kumar?
How much (does it cost)?	yem chizi tsumrer?
I don't eat meat.	uzesh gusht nei yowem
I'm lost.	mazhe hu fdek nost
Go away!	trabarech!

Useful Words

very	ghafeh
good/bad	baaf/shaak
left/right	chap/rost
this/that	yem/ya
here/there	drem/dra
market/shop	bozor/dukon
mountain/peak	kho/sar
river	darya
valley	zherav
guide	fdek disuv nikuz
north/south	shumaal/jnu
east/west	mashriq/maghrib

Family

man/woman	dai/hruinan
father/mother	taat/nun
husband/wife	shauhar/jamat
brother/sister	vrut/khuy
son/daughter	petr/theyght
friend	doost

Accommodation

hotel	hoteli
guesthouse	mehmonkhona

room	uchaak
bed	pipr
single/double room	yi/bu khaalgeh pipr
key	weshik
room	jayi
toilet	tarkank

Food

restaurant	shapik yiteh jai
apple	mur
apricot	chuan
egg	tukhmurgeh
food/bread	shapik
meat	gosht
rice	gerangeh
vegetable	ghazk
whole-wheat bread	kamishdoon dildungi
yoghurt	pai
milk	bursh
tea	choi
water	yupek

Time

What time is it?	tsumar wakhti vitk?
When?	tsoghdar?
today	wuthk
tomorrow	pigha
yesterday	yezi
now	niveh

Monday	dushambi	Friday	juma
Tuesday	sishambi	Saturday	shambi
Wednesday	chorshambi	Sunday	yekshambi
Thursday	panshambi		

THE SILK ROAD

Numbers

1	yiu	20	wist
2	bui	30	wista-thas
3	trui	40	buwist
4	tsebur	50	buwista-thas
5	panz	60	truwist
6	shal	70	truwista-thas
7	hoob	80	tseburwist
8	haat	90	tseburwista-thas
9	nau	100	saad
10	thas	1000	hazor

INDEX

KHOWAR 215

KOHISTANI 216

KYRGYZ 73

What kind of traveller are you?

A. You're eating chicken for dinner *again* because it's the only word you know.

B. When no one understands what you say, you step closer and shout louder.

C. When the barman doesn't understand your order, you point frantically at the beer.

D. You're surrounded by locals, swapping jokes, email addresses and experiences – other travellers want to borrow your phrasebook or audio guide.

If you answered A, B, or C, you NEED Lonely Planet's language products ...

- **Lonely Planet Phrasebooks** – for every phrase you need in every language you want
- **Lonely Planet Language & Culture** – get behind the scenes of English as it's spoken around the world – learn and laugh
- **Lonely Planet Fast Talk & Fast Talk Audio** – essential phrases for short trips and weekends away – read, listen and talk like a local
- **Lonely Planet Small Talk** – 10 essential languages for city breaks
- **Lonely Planet Real Talk** – downloadable language audio guides from lonelyplanet.com to your MP3 player

... and this is why

- **Talk to everyone everywhere**
  Over 120 languages, more than any other publisher
- **The right words at the right time**
  Quick-reference colour sections, two-way dictionary, easy pronunciation, every possible subject – and audio to support it

Lonely Planet Offices

Australia
90 Maribyrn   City Rd
Victoria 301   ²NT
☎ 03 8379 8000   ☎ 510 250 6400   ☎ 020 7106 2100
fax 03 8379 8111   fax 510 893 8572   fax 020 7106 2101
✉ talk2us@lonelyplanet.com.au   ✉ info@lonelyplanet.com   ✉ go@lonelyplanet.co.uk

31901046232635

lonelyplanet.com